BABY
COSTUMES

BABY COSTUMES

Bettine Roynon

MQP

Published by MQ Publications Limited

12 The Ivories
6–8 Northampton Street
London N1 2HY
Tel: +44 (020) 7359 2244
Fax: +44 (020) 7359 1616
E-mail: mail@mqpublications.com

North American Office
49 West 24th Street
8th Floor
New York, NY 10010
E-mail: information@mqpublicationsus.com

Web site: www.mqpublications.com

Copyright © 2006 MQ Publications Limited
Text copyright 2006 © Bettine Roynon

Photography: Lizzie Orme
Peapod, cabbage, and dragon photography: Jordan Elyse Photography
Illustrations: Claire Garland

ISBN 13: 978-1-84601-121-4
ISBN 10: 1-84601-121-3

1 3 5 7 9 0 8 6 4 2

Printed in Italy

contents

BUTTERFLY

YOU WILL NEED

To fit a child of around 10 months

- White cotton onesie with long sleeves and legs, and center front opening
- Dylon machine dye in Sunflower
- Adhesive tape
- Two 17 x 24-in. sheets of ¼-in. brown foam
- Tracing wheel
- Scalpel and cutting mat
- 20 in. of 36-in.-wide white silk habotai
- Medium paintbrushes
- Fabric adhesive
- Dylon fabric paints in Red and Yellow
- Dylon Shade Creator
- Needle and yellow thread
- Steam iron
- 20 in. of ¼-in.-wide black elastic

Tip: *Use your imagination to come up with a creative color pattern for the butterfly wings. You can use any number of vibrant colors to make the wings stand out, or subtle shades for a softer butterfly.*

1 Dye the onesie yellow according to the manufacturer's instructions. Leave to dry.

TO MAKE THE WINGS

2 Enlarge the template on page 136 so that it is approx. 14 in. in height. Tape it to the sheet of brown foam, keeping it at one end so you can flip it over along the dotted line to make the opposite half of the wing. Using a tracing wheel, trace along all the solid lines onto the foam. Do not trace along the dotted line.

3 Flip the template over on the dotted line to create the other half of the wing. Using the tracing wheel, trace along all the solid lines. You now have a pair of wings. Cut around the outline using a scalpel and cutting mat, then cut out the shapes for the pattern which are unshaded on the template.

Step 3

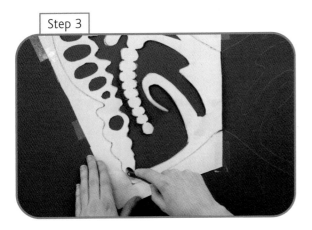

4 Place your pair of wings directly onto your second sheet of foam and, using them as a template, copy the design, then cut out. You now have two pairs of wings. Reserve a piece of foam to make the antennae.

5 Take one pair of wings. Cut a piece of habotai slightly larger than the wings. Using a paintbrush, apply a very thin layer of fabric adhesive to the foam (just enough to make the surface tacky) then gently lay the habotai on top, ensuring that it is taut and flat.

6 When the adhesive is almost dry, use a sharp scalpel to trim the habotai just inside the edge of the butterfly wings. Leave to dry completely.

Step 6

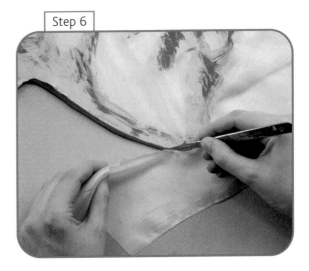

7 Keep the wings foam side down on the table. Paint the habotai with fabric paint in red and yellow where it covers the holes in the foam. Following the manufacturer's instructions, use the Shade Creator to soften the join between the colors and create a shaded effect. You can paint over all the habotai if you like, but the design will only appear through the holes in the foam. Don't use too much paint, however, otherwise the habotai will wrinkle. Leave to dry.

Step 8

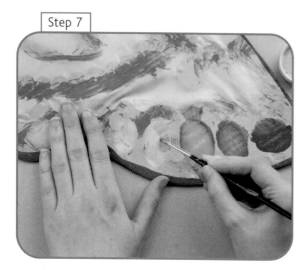

Step 7

8 Position the wings foam side down on the back of the onesie, making sure they are centered. Using large stitches, and catching just a small amount of onesie each time, hand stitch a rectangle approx. 1 in. wide in the center of the wings to attach them to the onesie.

9 Apply a thin layer of fabric adhesive to the second pair of wings and stick it on top of the first pair, making sure you line up the design carefully. Place the whole wing area under a few heavy books until dry.

TO MAKE THE ANTENNAE

10 Using the template on page 136, cut the shape out from some remaining brown foam. Cut along the internal lines as indicated on the template. Curl the ends of the antennae around a pencil, take a hot steam iron, and direct steam toward the foam at a safe distance of about 16 in. away. This helps to curl the foam. Wait until foam is completely cool before releasing.

11 Insert elastic through the two slots at the bottom of the hairband. Place the hairband around the child's head to establish the length of elastic you need. Tie off the elastic and cut off any excess.

SOLAR SYSTEM

YOU WILL NEED

To fit a child of around 3 years

- White cotton onesie with long sleeves and legs, and center front opening
- Dylon machine dye in Indigo
- White cotton pull-on hat
- Dylon machine dye in Burnt Orange
- Dylon 3D fabric paint in Glow In The Dark
- Small paintbrush
- Stippling or stencil brush
- Dylon fabric paints in White, Red, Turquoise, Green, Navy, Yellow, Bronze, and Silver
- Dylon Image Maker or Image Maker inkjet transfer paper (optional)
- 5 styrofoam balls, approx. 3 in. in diameter
- White acrylic primer
- 80 in. of black plastic boning strip
- Scissors
- Needle and black and gray thread, or sewing machine
- Scraps of fabric in the colors of your planets, or scraps of white fabric painted to match the colors of your planets
- Fabric adhesive
- Masking tape
- Three 8 x 12-in. sheets of ¼-in. orange foam
- 10 in. of 45-in.-wide orange organza
- One pair of gray panty hose
- 1-lb. bag of polyester fiberfill stuffing

1 Dye the onesie indigo according to the manufacturer's instructions. Leave to dry.

2 Dye the hat orange according to the manufacturer's instructions. Leave to dry.

TO DECORATE THE ONESIE

3 Dot the onesie all over with glow in the dark paint to create stars.

4 Stipple white fabric paint diagonally across the front of the onesie to create a milky way effect.

Step 4

5 Paint a large swirl on the back of the onesie to represent a galaxy, using the fabric paints. If you don't feel confident painting the shape freehand, photocopy an astronomical picture and use Image Maker to transfer it to the onesie, according to the manufacturer's instructions.

TO MAKE THE PLANETS

6 Paint the styrofoam balls with primer. Leave to dry, then paint in various colors with the fabric paints. Leave to dry.

7 Measure your child's waist. Cut a piece of boning three times this measure.

15

8 Overlap the two ends of boning by about 1 in. and stitch them together by hand or with a zigzag stitch on the sewing machine to make a large hoop. Twist the hoop into a figure-of-eight and stitch where it crosses. Fold one half hoop over the other and stitch together again directly opposite the first crossover point.

9 Glue the planets with fabric adhesive onto the hoops. To provide extra security, glue a strip of fabric the same color as the planet across the boning. Twist the boning so that it curves all around the planet and secure with masking tape. This will help keep the planet in place while the adhesive is drying. Leave to dry.

10 Stitch one of the crossover points onto the center back of the onesie through both hoops. Then sew one hoop to one side seam of the onesie, and the other to the opposite side seam.

Step 9

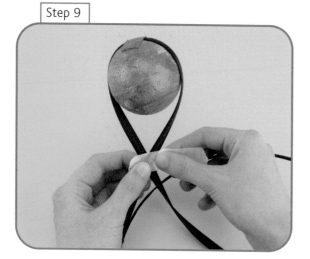

TO MAKE THE HAT

11 Cut eight isosceles triangles with a base of approx. 3 in. out of the orange foam. Cut four slightly larger triangles of organza and glue a layer of organza between two layers of foam.

12 Glue the four triangles vertically in a line across the top of the hat. Leave to dry overnight.

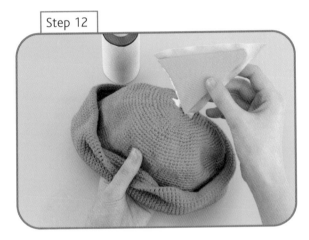

Step 12

TO MAKE THE ANKLE CUFFS

13 Cut the legs off the panty hose, then cut four 8-in. lengths of tube from the legs. Fill each tube with fiberfill stuffing then bend into a donut shape and stitch the edges closed, tucking the raw edges inside as you sew.

14 Paint each cuff with silver fabric paint. Leave to dry.

17

PEAPOD

YOU WILL NEED

To fit a child of around 3 months

- White cotton onesie with long sleeves, no legs, and no center front opening
- White cotton pull-on hat
- 6 x 12-in. piece of white cotton jersey
- Dylon machine dye in Lime
- Pencil
- Scissors
- Needle and green thread or sewing machine
- 1-lb. bag of polyester fiberfill stuffing
- Dylon fabric paint in Green
- Dylon Shade Creator
- 40 in. of 45-in.-wide green brushed cotton
- 20 in. of 50-in.-wide lightweight batting
- Fabric adhesive
- Paintbrush
- 2 old jars or glasses
- Masking tape

1 Dye the onesie, hat, and jersey lime green according to the manufacturer's instructions. Leave to dry.

TO MAKE THE PEAS

2 In the center of the piece of jersey, draw two circles, approx. 5½ in. in diameter, just touching one another.

3 Lay the piece of jersey on the center front of the onesie and machine stitch along the line round both circles, using a very short zigzag stitch. If you are hand sewing, use a short backstitch. Make sure you only sew the front layer of the onesie without catching the back layer. Cut away excess fabric close to the circle seams.

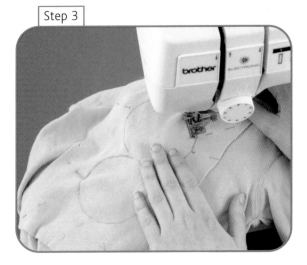

Step 3

4 Turn the onesie inside out, and cut a small slit in the onesie fabric at the center of each circle. Only cut the onesie, not the jersey circles. Push fiberfill stuffing through the slit and into the circle to create the peas. Fill to maximum capacity—you want the peas to be as puffy and firm as possible. Hand stitch the slit closed.

5 Turn the onesie right side out again. Using green fabric paint, paint some deeper color around the base of the peas. Use the Shade Creator according the manufacturer's instructions to shade the color lighter toward the top, making the peas look more three-dimensional.

TO MAKE THE POD

6 Enlarge the template on page 137 so that it is 30 in. between the red dots, and use it to cut out four layers of green brushed cotton and two layers of batting. Place two pieces of cotton right sides together and lay a piece of the batting on top. Stitch along the straight edge through all the layers, then trim away as much batting as you can from the seam allowance.

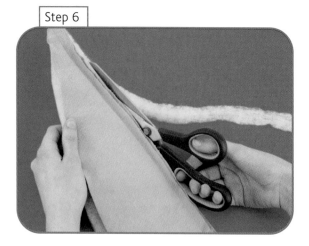

Step 6

7 Fold over the top layer of cotton to sandwich the batting. Press seam. This is one side of the pod.

8 To make the other side of the pod, place the remaining layers of cotton right sides together and lay the last piece of batting on top. Stitch along the straight edge through all the layers, then trim away the batting from the seam allowance. Repeat step 7.

9 Lay the two sides of the pod together on top of one another, right sides together, with the seam to the left and the unfinished raw edges to the right.

10 Fold back just the top and bottom layers of cotton to the left, so they are right sides together, with the raw edges lined up all around and the seam now in the middle.

11 Starting on the two layers of cotton to the left, stitch a seam around the pod shape along the raw edges. Pivot at the points of the pod, and on the second half stitch through both layers of cotton and batting. When you get back to where you started, leave an opening approx. 6 in. long.

12 Pull the pod right side outward through the opening. Press seams and stitch the opening closed.

13 Cut a leaf shape out of two layers of green cotton. Holding the two leaves exactly together, stitch along the length and across the width to mimic leaf veins.

14 Mix one part adhesive with four parts water. Using a paintbrush, coat the leaf with the adhesive mixture. Wrap the wet leaf around two jars or glasses to create a wavy shape, hold in place with masking tape, and leave to dry overnight. Hand sew the leaf onto the tip of the pod.

Step 14

FLAMINGO

YOU WILL NEED

To fit a child of around 2 years

- 60 in. of 45-in.-wide pink organza
- Needle and pink thread
- 10 in. of 54-in.-wide pink netting
- Sewing machine
- 40 in. of ½-in.-wide white elastic
- 2 pairs of pink panty hose
- 1-lb. bag of polyester fiberfill stuffing
- Dylon fabric paint in Black
- Fine paintbrush
- Metal snap (two-part set for hand sewing)
- Scrap of pink organza or satin ribbon, tied into a bow (optional)
- Pink dance leotard

Tip: *If you like, you can hide the metal snap at the base of the flamingo neck by stitching on a ribbon bow.*

TO MAKE THE SKIRT

1 Cut a length of organza 60 x 20 in. and fold in half across the width, right sides together. Stitch the two short sides together.

2 Turn the fabric right side out, then fold it in half lengthwise so the two long raw edges are together and you now have four layers. Sandwich a length of rumpled-up netting inside to create a puffy tube.

3 Keeping the raw edges together, run a gathering stitch along their full length, either by hand or using the longest stitch length on the sewing machine. This will be the top of the skirt.

4 Measure your child's waist. Cut a piece of elastic the same length as this measurement, then overlap the two ends by 1 in. and stitch them together firmly.

5 Stretch the elastic circle out to its full length and measure the circumference it will stretch to. Gather the top of the skirt to match this dimension. Pin the elastic to the skirt at center front, center back, and side seams.

Step 5

6 Using a zigzag stitch on the machine, sew the gathered top of the skirt onto the elastic, stretching the elastic out as you work. Trim any excess fabric away from the waistband to neaten it up.

7 Gather three 1-in.-deep pleats across the front of the skirt about halfway up and stitch in place. This will make the front of the skirt shorter than the back.

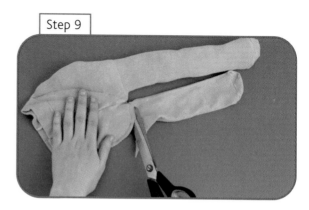

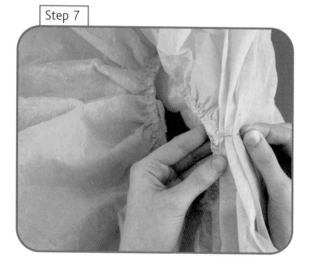

TO MAKE THE FLAMINGO NECK

8 Take one of the pairs of pink panty hose and stuff one leg with fiberfill stuffing to make a long neck shape. Stitch across the top of the leg in a curved line, then stitch across the top of the other leg in the same curve.

9 Cut off the unstuffed leg and trim close to the seam line. The body of the panty hose will then form a rounded cap to fit over the child's head.

10 Paint the tip of the stuffed leg black, where it joins the hat, to make a beak.

11 Hand stitch one half of the snap onto the base of the stuffed leg. Stitch the second half of the snap to the top of the leotard at center back. If the leg of the panty hose is long enough, you can stitch it to the back of the skirt instead.

GOLDFISH

YOU WILL NEED

To fit a child of around 11 months

- White cotton onesie with long sleeves and legs, and center front opening
- White cotton pull-on hat
- Dylon machine dye in Burnt Orange
- Piece of scrap cardboard
- Dylon fabric paint in Gold and Fluorescent Orange
- Small paintbrush
- Scrap of cotton cloth about 16 in. square
- Iron
- Scissors
- 5¾ yd. of 1 to 1½-in.-wide orange ribbon
- 5¾ yd. of 1 to 1½-in.-wide yellow ribbon
- Dressmaker's pins
- Needle and orange thread
- 40 in. of 45-in.-wide orange tulle or organza
- 40 in. of 45-in.-wide yellow tulle or organza

Tip: *It is easier to pleat the lengths of ribbon for the fish scales if at least one of your ribbons is wired craft ribbon. Just make sure the wire is turned in at the ends so that there is no risk of scratching the child.*

1 Dye the onesie and hat orange according to the manufacturer's instructions. Leave to dry.

TO DECORATE THE ONESIE

2 Lay the onesie front side up on a table, with a piece of scrap cardboard between the front and back. Paint fish scales on the front with gold and orange fabric paint. Leave to dry.

Step 2

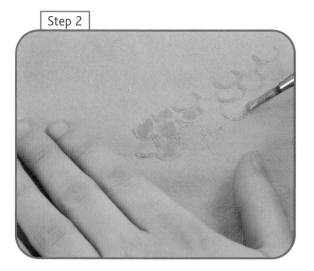

3 Cover the design with the piece of scrap cloth and press with a dry iron on a medium heat.

4 Cut a 40-in. length of orange ribbon and the same of yellow. Place them on a table so that the ends overlap and the ribbons lie at right angles to each other. Pin in place to keep the ends together as you work. Fold the bottom ribbon across the top one and lie it flat again in the opposite direction, still at right angles to the other ribbon. Repeat with the other ribbon, then keep going until the full lengths of both ribbons are folded into one square.

Step 4

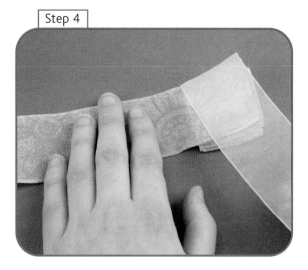

5 Repeat Step 4 four more times so that you have five lengths of folded ribbon. Hold the ribbons at one end and pull the other end so they stretch out like a concertina. These are your fish scales for the back of the onesie.

6 Position these five lengths of ribbon side by side on the back of the onesie in a fish shape (so that they are narrower at the neck and bottom but swell out at the body). Leave tail ends of ribbons hanging at the bottom temporarily. Securely stitch each ribbon onto the onesie at intervals of 2 in.

7 Cut an oval 5 in. long and 3 in. wide from paper and use this as a template for the belly and hat fins. Enlarge the tail template on page 137 so that it is approx. 25½ in. long. Cut two layers of each colored tulle or organza for the tail fin and two layers of each for the two hat and the two belly fins. Place all the tail fins on top of one another.

8 Pinch the tail fins at the center and tie with thread to hold shape.

9 Going back to the fish scales, divide the ribbon tails so that you have equal amounts on each side, insert the tail fins and tie ribbon tails firmly around them where they have been pinched.

Step 9

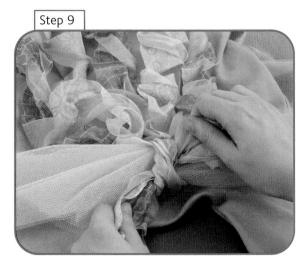

10 Securely stitch the tail fins in place and trim the ribbon tails at an angle so that they don't fray.

11 Pair together an orange and yellow belly fin, fold the pair down the center, and run a gathering stitch along the fold line. Gather to approx. 1$\frac{1}{2}$ in. Do not trim the thread ends.

12 Using the gathering thread, sew the fins onto the belly of the onesie on one edge of the painted scales.

13 Repeat step 11 for the second pair of belly fins and sew onto the other edge of the painted scales.

TO MAKE THE HAT
14 Pair together an orange and yellow hat fin, fold the pair along the center, and run a gathering stitch along the fold line. Gather to 1$\frac{1}{4}$ in. Do not trim the thread ends.

15 Using the gathering thread, sew the hat fins onto one side seam of the hat. If they look too much like ears, baste the bottom layer of the fin onto the hat to hold it in place.

16 Repeat step 14 for the second pair of hat fins and sew onto the other side seam of the hat.

OWL

YOU WILL NEED

To fit a child of around 2 years

- 1¼ yd. of 62-in.-wide faux fur
- Scissors
- Dressmaker's chalk
- Sewing machine
- Bag of small feathers to contrast with the faux fur
- Fabric adhesive
- 1¼ yd. of 62-in.-wide satin in a color to blend with the faux fur
- 1¼ yd. of 1½-in.-wide satin or organza ribbon to match satin fabric
- Freezer paper
- Scrap of gray foam or felt
- ½ yd. of 2-in.-wide elastic
- White onesie with long sleeves, no legs, and no center front opening

Tip: *To cut faux fur, place reverse side up and use only the tip of the scissors to make small snips or use a scalpel. This minimizes the risk of damaging the fur.*

TO MAKE THE CAPE

1 Enlarge the template on page 138 so that the distance between the two red dots on the template matches the distance between your child's head and knees. Make sure the fur pile runs down toward the base of the cape then cut out the first piece of the cape. Mark the notches, as indicated on the template, around the edge with chalk.

2 Flip the template over and cut out the second piece of the cape. Make sure you mirror any markings from the first side of the faux fur.

3 With right sides together, sew the two pieces of fur together along center back, lining up the notches. On right side, brush the seam to pull out any fur caught in it.

4 Take some long feathers, lift up the fur on the hood where the cross is marked on the template, and position about three feathers in the opposite direction to the fur so that they stick up. Sew firmly in place at the base of the feather and reinforce the stitching with a drop of adhesive. Leave to dry. Brush the fur over the base of the feather to conceal the stitching and adhesive.

5 Randomly along the back of the cape, place feathers in the direction of fur and sew firmly into place. Reinforce each feather with a drop of adhesive. Leave to dry then test each feather to check that it is securely fastened.

Step 5

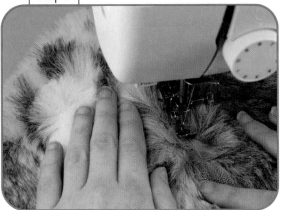

6 Fold the satin in half lengthwise right sides together and, using the same template as in step 1, cut out the lining shape as indicated on the template. Mark the notches around the edge.

7 Cut the ribbon in half. Match the cape and the lining, right sides together, lining up any notches. Where indicated on the template, insert the ribbon so $3/8$ in. is protruding and the rest of the ribbon is sandwiched between the layers. Pin in place.

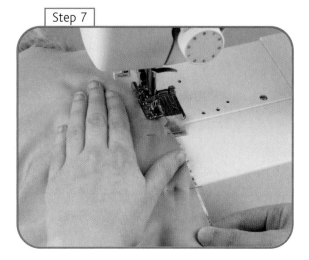

Step 7

8 Enlarge the peak template on page 138 so that it is 2 in. wide. Cut from the gray foam or felt and insert it between the cape and the lining at the front of the hood, where marked on the template, so that a triangle shape protrudes. Pin in place.

9 Starting at the bottom, stitch all around the cape, leaving an opening approx. 10 in. long when you get back to the bottom.

10 Turn the cape right side out through the opening. Hand stitch across the base of the triangle to hold it in position. Stitch the opening closed.

TO MAKE THE SPATS
11 On the reverse side of the faux fur, draw two identical spats in the shape of a rectangle which has one curved longer edge. The longer straight edge of the segments should measure approx. $9^1/_2$ in. Measure your child's ankle and cut two pieces of elastic slightly smaller.

12 Sandwich one spat (fur side down) between a small sheet of freezer paper and the elastic—this will stop the fur getting caught in the sewing machine. Using a zigzag stitch, sew the elastic down the straight edge of the spat, stretching the elastic as you work. You need to end up with around $^3/_8$ in. of elastic protruding on each side of the spat.

Step 12

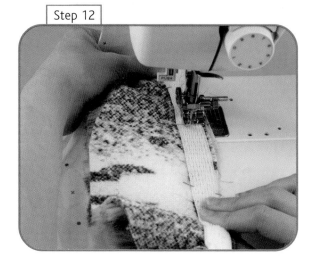

13 With right sides of the faux fur together, overlap the two ends of elastic and stitch them together on each side of the spat. Turn right side out. Repeat steps 12 and 13 for the other spat.

CATERPILLAR

YOU WILL NEED

To fit a child of around 5 months

- White cotton onesie with long sleeves
- 10 in. of 60-in.-wide white jersey
- Dylon machine dye in Burnt Orange
- Scissors
- 1¼ yd. of 40-in.-wide pale green fleece
- Dressmaker's transfer paper in contrasting color to fleece
- Tracing wheel
- Needle and green thread
- 20 in. of 36-in.-wide pale blue tulle
- 20 in. of 36-in.-wide dark blue tulle
- 10 orange pom-poms
- Sewing machine
- 2 yd. of thin cord or ribbon
- Iron
- Small paintbrush
- Dylon fabric paint in Bronze

Tip: *The pom-poms are stitched to just one side of this costume. Simply swivel the costume round so the pom-poms are on the back if your baby wants to lie on his or her front.*

1 Dye the onesie and jersey orange according to the manufacturer's instructions. Leave to dry.

TO MAKE THE BODY OF THE CATERPILLAR
2 Enlarge the template on page 138 so that it is 26 in. long from top to bottom, lay on the fleece, then cut three pieces of fleece (two for the front and one for the back).

3 Lay one piece of fleece right side up on the colored transfer paper. Place the template on top, matching the edges. Mark all the lines and markings from the template onto the reverse of the fleece by pressing hard with the tracing wheel.

4 Baste along the center line and all the lines running from right to left so you can see them on the right side. Cut a small "+" where indicated in each of the rectangles.

5 Place the marked fleece down, wrong side up, and lay the two pieces of tulle over it, one on top of the other. Push a pom-pom into the tulle and through each "+." Turn the whole thing over carefully and check that each pom-pom looks good on the right side.

Step 5

6 Trim any excess tulle from around the edges, but leave an extra 1½ in. all around as a seam allowance.

7 Take a second piece of fleece and lay it down on top of the pom-pomed fleece, with right sides together and matching the sides.

8 Being careful to trap the layers of tulle in the seam, stitch along one long edge, stopping at the bottom horizontal basting line. Stitch round the armholes and neck edge. Turn right side out through the unfinished side and press seams gently.

9 Top stitch along each basting line sewing through both layers. Remove basting stitch.

10 Lay the last piece of fleece (which will be the back of the caterpillar) right sides together on top of the pom-pomed fleece. Stitch down the unfinished side seam and all around the bottom stopping at the finished edge. Also sew all along the shoulders.

11 Trim away any excess tulle in the seams, but leave the fleece seam allowance to stop the tulle scratching the child. Turn right side out.

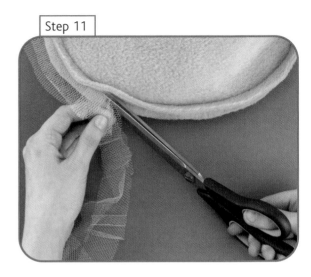

Step 11

TO MAKE THE CATERPILLAR LEGS

12 Cut two long strips of jersey 2 in. wide and across the full width of the fabric. Fold one strip in half along its length, right sides together and sandwiching the cord or ribbon between the layers. Stitch across one short end to hold the cord securely in place.

13 Machine stitch down the length with a $^3/_8$-in. seam allowance. Use a small stitch length and make sure you don't catch the cord at any point by pushing it as far against the fold as possible.

14 Trim off the top but leave the seam allowance to help bulk out the interior of the piping once you have pulled it through.

15 Pull on the free end of the cord and gently coax the tip of the jersey tube to turn in on itself. As the tube turns right side out, the seams will be on the inside and you will have a length of piping. (See step 10 on page 65.) Cut the end off the jersey and remove cord. Repeat with the other length of jersey. From the two lengths of piping cut ten pieces 3½ in. long, and five pieces 7 in. long.

16 Returning to the fleece bag, take five of the shorter leg ties and pin one at the end of each line of top stitching down the open side of the front. Hand stitch in place on the inside.

17 On the back panel, turn the remaining raw edge in by ½ in. to the wrong side and press in place to hold. Pin the other five ties to the back down this edge, matching the position of the top ties. Sew along the turned over seam, catching the leg ties as you go.

18 Fold the five longer leg ties in half and hand stitch through the fold to the seam on the other side of the bag, placing one at the end of each line of top stitching. Tie each one in a knot.

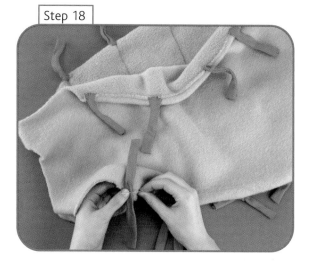

Step 18

19 Paint a line along each top stitching line using bronze fabric paint. Leave to dry.

SNOWFLAKE

YOU WILL NEED

To fit a child of around 2 years

- 1¼ yd. of 54-in.-wide dark blue tulle
- 1¼ yd. of 54-in.-wide light blue tulle
- 1¼ yd. of 54-in.-wide turquoise tulle
- Scissors
- Thin cotton shorts in blue, with elasticated waist, to fit your child
- ¾ yd. of 1-in.-wide elastic
- Dressmaker's pins
- Sewing machine
- Sheet of paper at least 27 in. square
- Pencil
- ¾ yd. of 72-in.-wide dark blue felt
- Small scissors or scalpel
- Dylon fabric paint in Turquoise, White, and Royal Blue
- Paintbrush
- Small piece of firm card
- Stippling or stencil brush
- Needle and blue thread
- Blue panty hose to fit your child
- Pale blue T-shirt or leotard to fit your child

Tip: *If you don't have a stencil brush, take a regular, fat paintbrush and cut straight across the tip of the bristles.*

TO MAKE THE SKIRT

1 Cut a 19½-in. square from paper. In the center, cut out a circle 9½ in. in diameter. This is the template for the large skirt shape. Cut a 15½-in. square from paper. In the center, cut out a circle 9½ in. in diameter. This is the template for the small skirt shape. Cut one large and one small skirt shape out of each of the three colored tulles.

2 Cut a length of elastic slightly larger than the waist measurement of the shorts, overlap the ends, and stitch together.

3 Place the layers of tulle one on top of the other, matching edges at the waist, but allowing the points to stick out in different directions.

4 Pin the waist of the layers of tulle onto one edge of the elastic at front, back, and both sides. The raw edges of the tulle should be flush with the edge of the elastic, although the waist measurement will be longer than the circle of elastic.

5 Machine stitch the tulle layers to the elastic, using a zigzag stitch and stretching the elastic as much as possible. When you have finished, the tulle skirt will be gathered to a slightly larger waist size than the shorts.

6 To make the snowflake pattern for the felt skirt, fold the 27-in. square piece of paper in half, then quarters, then fold it again diagonally from the center point. Enlarge the snowflake template on page 139 so that it is 9 in. between the red dots and lay it on top of the folded paper. Draw the pattern onto the paper, cut along the outline, and cut out the areas unshaded on the template. Unfold the paper.

7 Using the large skirt template from step 1, cut the top skirt from the blue felt. Lay the paper snowflake pattern on top and trace the design onto the felt. Cut the shapes out with small scissors or a scalpel.

8 Using white fabric paint and the regular paintbrush, paint the edge and around the center of the snowflake. Use quite a dry brush and aim your brushstrokes inward so that the white is graded.

9 Sew the felt skirt onto the elastic above the tulle, with the seam allowance pointing up to hide the edges of the tulle and the elastic.

Step 9

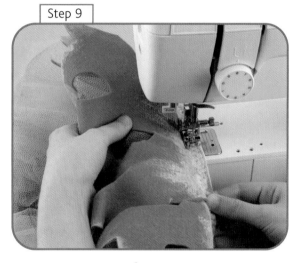

10 Hand stitch the skirt just below the waistband of the shorts at center front and back, and at both side seams. By only stitching at a few points the elastic of both the shorts and skirt will maintain its stretch. The skirt should sit on the hips, not at the waist.

TO DECORATE THE PANTY HOSE

11 Make your own snowflake stencils from strong paper. Push a small piece of firm card down the leg of the panty hose to prevent any paint bleeding through them, then stencil snowflakes with royal blue and turquoise fabric paint onto the panty hose. Use a dry stencil brush to prevent any bleeding.

TO DECORATE THE T-SHIRT

12 Using leftover tulle, fold small pieces into eighths (as in step 6) and cut simple snowflake patterns.

Step 12

13 Baste the tulle snowflakes randomly all over the T-shirt. To do this, gather the snowflake and T-shirt in the fist of your hand and sew the center of the snowflake a number of times. This prevents the thread from getting caught up in the tulle.

Step 13

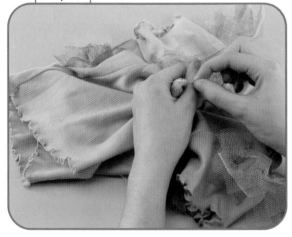

14 Take two snowflakes and sew them onto each shoulder of the T-shirt to create little epaulets.

TURTLE

YOU WILL NEED

To fit a child of around 12 months

- White cotton onesie with long sleeves and legs, and center front opening
- Dylon machine dye in Green
- Large brown adult hat with floppy brim and no seams
- Bowl, slightly larger than the hat
- Steam iron
- Clothes pegs
- 1-lb. bag of polyester fiberfill stuffing
- Dressmaker's pins
- 20-in. square of green upholstery fabric or vinyl
- Scissors
- Fabric adhesive
- Needle and brown thread

Tip: *Use upholstery fabric or vinyl for the pattern on the turtle shell to create a good textured effect. If you can't find any, simply use felt which won't fray when you cut it.*

1 Dye the onesie green according to the manufacturer's instructions. Leave to dry.

2 Remove any lining ribbon or decorations from the hat.

3 Wet the hat with hot water and shape over the overturned bowl. Use steam from a hot iron to stretch and shape the hat into a smooth shape. When you get a turtle-shell shape, peg the hat to the sides of the bowl and leave to dry overnight.

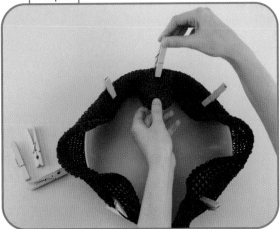

Step 3

4 Remove the bowl and fill the hat with fiberfill stuffing—just enough to fill but not overstuff it.

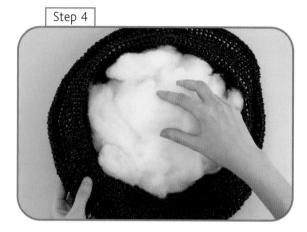

Step 4

5 Pin the hat onto the back of the onesie so that you leave approx. 2 in. of the hat free.

6 Cut out round-edged shapes from the upholstery fabric or vinyl. Glue them as desired onto the hat.

7 Sew the hat onto the onesie by catching just a small amount of onesie fabric with the needle. This ensures that the onesie can stretch once it is on the child.

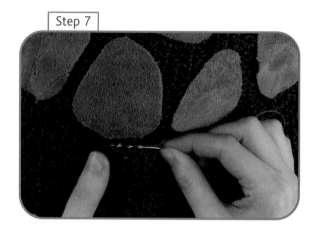

Step 7

HONEYCOMB

YOU WILL NEED

To fit a child of around 11 months

- White cotton onesie with long sleeves and legs, and center front opening
- White cotton pull-on hat
- Dylon machine dye in Sunflower
- Large potato, or even better, a yam
- Scalpel or sharp knife
- Paper towels
- Dylon fabric paint in Gold and Red
- Medium paintbrush
- Scrap of cotton cloth around 16-in. square
- Iron
- 8 in. of ⅛-in.-wide black elastic
- Four small yellow pom-poms
- 10-in.-square piece of yellow tulle
- Needle and yellow thread
- One 8 x 12-in. sheet of ¼-in. yellow foam
- One 17 x 24-in. sheet of ¼-in. yellow foam
- Fabric adhesive

Tip: *Make sure the bees are very firmly sewn on as children are likely to try to pull them off!*

1 Dye the onesie and hat yellow according to the manufacturer's instructions. Leave to dry.

2 Cut the potato or yam in half. Draw a hexagon on the potato flesh and cut out the flesh around the hexagon carefully with a scalpel or knife to make a stamp.

3 Allow the potato to dry, face down on paper towel, for 10–15 minutes.

4 Paint the stamp with gold fabric paint and two edges with a light coat of red. The red will seep into the gold and provide a subtle darker shade around the edges of the stamp.

Step 4

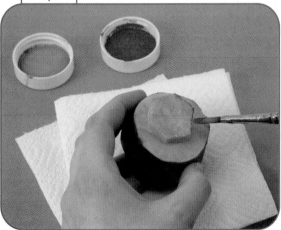

5 Starting at the top of the onesie, begin stamping honeycomb design, working your way down. Stamp back, sleeves, and soles of onesie too. Leave to dry.

Step 5

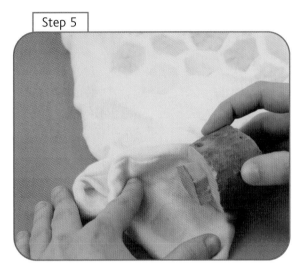

6 Use the scrap of cotton cloth to protect the design and press with a dry iron on a medium heat for two minutes to set the paint.

TO MAKE THE BEES

7 Cut the elastic into 2-in. lengths. Wind two pieces round each yellow pom-pom and tie off securely at the bottom. Trim the ends of the elastic so they look like little legs.

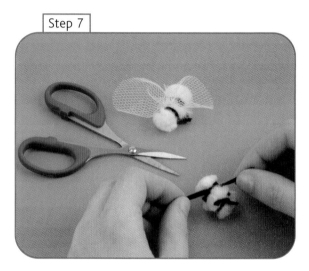

Step 7

8 Cut five pieces of yellow tulle approx. 1 x 2½ in. and trim the short ends so that they are curved. Take one piece, pinch it in the middle, and sew onto the pom-pom to create wings. Using the same thread, attach the bees securely to the onesie and hat randomly. Pass the needle through the elastic stripes for extra security.

TO MAKE THE HAT

9 Cut a dripping honey shape from the smaller yellow foam sheet and glue onto the hat. Leave the hat to dry inside out to help hold the foam shape in place.

TO MAKE THE HONEYCOMB WINGS

10 Enlarge the wing template on page 139 so it is 8$\frac{1}{2}$ in. long. Tape it to the larger sheet of yellow foam, keeping it at one end so you can flip it over along the dotted line to make the opposite half of the wing. Trace along all the solid lines onto the foam. Do not trace along the dotted line. Flip the template over on the dotted line and trace the other half of the wing. Cut out the whole wing shape.

11 Place the wings on the back of the onesie and stitch in place along the center back in a rectangle about 1 in. wide using long stitches. You can also pipe a thin line of adhesive close along the stitching to secure it.

61

LOBSTER

YOU WILL NEED

To fit a child of around 2 years

- White cotton onesie with long sleeves and legs, and center front opening
- White cotton pull-on hat
- Dylon machine dye in Poppy Red
- 1¼ yd. of 40-in.-wide red fleece
- Dressmaker's chalk
- Scissors
- Needle and red thread or sewing machine
- 1-lb. bag of polyester fiberfill stuffing
- Padded sleeveless vest in red with center front zipper
- 1¼ yd. of thin cord or ribbon
- 8 x 12-in. sheet of ¼-in. red foam
- 2 black pom-poms

Tip: *Save time by buying a red onesie and hat and skipping step 1.*

1 Dye the onesie and hat red according to the manufacturer's instructions. Leave to dry.

TO MAKE THE CLAWS

2 Cut two pieces of fleece 9 x 12 in. Fold each piece right sides together along the width. Using the template on page 140, draw a claw shape on the top layer with chalk.

3 Still with right sides together, stitch each claw all around the edge, leaving an opening at the wrist. Trim close to the seam then turn right side out and fill to capacity with fiberfill stuffing.

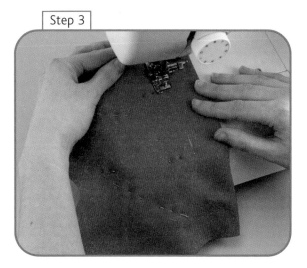

Step 3

4 Hand stitch the opening closed. Sew the claws onto the outside sleeve cuffs of the onesie.

TO MAKE THE BODY

5 Cut a piece of fleece 15 x 24 in. and fold it right sides together along the width. Enlarge the tail template on page 140 so that the long, straight edge matches the distance from side seam to side seam at the back, bottom hem of the sleeveless vest. Cut the tail shape through both layers of the fleece. Stitch together at the sides leaving top and bottom open.

6 Turn the tail right side out and fill with a small amount of stuffing. Stitch parallel lines from side seam to side seam as indicated on the template.

7 Using scissors, cut a fringe along the bottom edge of the tail as indicated on the template. Place the top of the tail inside the bottom hem of the sleeveless vest at the back and stitch along the hem to hold it in place.

Step 7

8 To make the little side legs for the sleeveless vest, cut a strip of fleece 1¼ yd. x 2 in., with the stretch running across the width. Fold the strip in half lengthwise, right sides together.

9 Place the length of cord between the layers of fleece, tight to the fold. Stitch across one short end to hold the cord in place. Stitch down the length of fleece, making sure not to catch the cord as you sew.

10 Pull on the free end of the cord and gently coax the tip of the fleece tube to turn in on itself. As the tube turns right side out, the seams will be on the inside and you will have a length of piping. Cut the end off the fleece and remove the cord.

Step 10

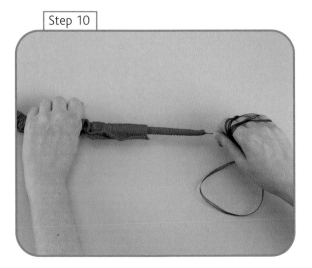

11 Cut the piping into six 4-in. lengths and sew these onto the side seams of the vest, three per side, and evenly spaced.

TO MAKE THE HAT

12 Cut two thin strips of red foam about 10 in. long and hand stitch one to each side of the hat. Angle the strips slightly so that they point to the back. Reinforce with a little adhesive. Glue and sew pom-poms onto the front of the hat for eyes.

MERMAID

YOU WILL NEED

To fit a child of around 10 months

- White cotton onesie with no sleeves or legs, and no center front opening
- Dylon machine dye in Green
- 10 in. of 45-in-wide green or blue organza
- Scissors
- 45-in. square iridescent taffeta in green-blue
- Pencil
- Sewing machine
- Reel of elastic sewing thread
- Dressmaker's pins
- 10 in. of $7/8$-in.-wide elastic

Tip: *If you have an active child who likes to get up and stand, you can adapt this costume to give more flexibility. Simply cut a neat slit at the base of the tail, round the back. This costume is not suitable for walking toddlers, however, as movement is extremely restricted.*

1 Dye the onesie green according to the manufacturer's instructions. Leave to dry.

TO MAKE THE TAIL

2 Cut a strip of organza on the bias, 10 x 1¼ in. Run a gathering stitch along one long edge. This will be the back fin.

3 On the right side of the taffeta square draw curved, parallel lines 1½ in. apart, diagonally across the square. Curving the lines will enable them to match up when you fold the fabric over in step 7.

4 Wind a sewing machine bobbin with elastic sewing thread by hand, stretching the elastic slightly as you work. Insert the bobbin back into the machine and set the stitch length to maximum.

5 With the right side of the fabric uppermost, machine stitch along the curved lines. Refill the bobbin with elastic as needed. If the fabric is not ruching, the elastic is probably not stretched enough on the bobbin.

6 Lay the gathered edge of the back fin along one edge of the ruched fabric, matching raw edges and with the width of the fin lying on top of the ruching. Pin in place. It does not matter if the fin is shorter than the ruching.

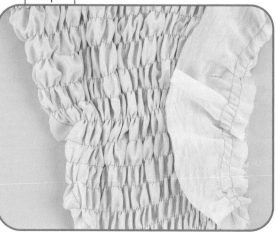

Step 6

69

7 Fold two adjacent edges of the ruched fabric over to make a cone, right sides together, matching ruched lines as much as possible. The organza back fin should run along one of the edges that you fold over. Stitch the seam, catching the back fin at the same time, which should end around 4 in. from the point of the cone.

8 Lay the cone flat with the seam on top and in the center. Measure the length of your child's legs. Trim the excess fabric off in a straight line at the top edge of the cone and cut the tip of the cone off at an angle into a neat "V" shape, making sure the cone is 5 in. longer than your child's leg measurement. Each side of the "V" should be approx. 3 in.

9 Enlarge the tail fin template on page 139 so that it is approx. 11 in. across the straight edge, and cut four tail fins from organza. Gather each fin to 3 in.

10 Insert two tail fins inside the opening in the bottom of the tail, lining up the gathered edge with one edge of the "V" shape. Pin in place then stitch. Repeat to stitch the other two tail fins on the other edge of the "V" shape.

11 Pull the cone right side out and make sure the tail fins and the back fin are all sitting nicely.

Step 10

12 Measure waist of child and cut a length of elastic to equal this measure. Overlap the ends of the elastic by about 1 in., then sew together.

13 Pin the elastic on the right side of the waist opening at the top of the tail at center front, center back, and at each side. Machine stitch in place along the bottom edge, using a zigzag stitch and stretching the elastic between the pins as you work.

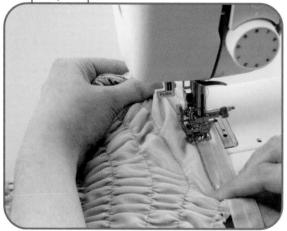

Step 13

14 Turn the elastic over so it is now inside the tail. Sew along the edge that is now at the bottom, again using zigzag stitch and stretching the elastic as you work.

TO MAKE THE ARM FINS

15 Enlarge the arm fin template on page 139 so that it is approx. 15½ in. along the straight edge and cut two arm fins from the organza. Gather each fin along the curved edge to approx. 4½ in.

16 Sew an arm fin onto the back edge of each armhole on the onesie, so that the main part of the fin points toward the center back. Fold the fins forward and press in place— this will make them stick out behind the child's shoulders.

DRAGON

YOU WILL NEED

To fit a child of around 15 months

- White cotton onesie with long sleeves and legs, and center front opening
- White cotton hooded cardigan
- Dylon machine dye in Burnt Orange
- Three 12 x 17-in. sheets of ¼-in. yellow foam
- Dylon fabric paint in Fluorescent Orange
- Scalpel and cutting mat
- Fabric adhesive
- 10 in. of 45-in.-wide orange organza, cut into two pieces 10 x 17 in. each
- 17 in. of 45-in.-wide red organza, cut into four pieces 10 x 17 in. each
- Medium paintbrush
- Scissors
- Needle and orange thread

Tip: *If you can't find a yellow foam sheet big enough to fit the whole spine and tail shape, cut the shape from two large sheets as indicated on the template and stitch each piece of spine to the hooded cardigan separately.*

1 Dye the onesie and cardigan with the orange machine dye according to the manufacturer's instructions. Leave to dry.

2 Enlarge the templates on page 141 so that the spine and tail shape is 39 in. long and the wing is approx. 9 in. across. Cut a spine and tail shape and four wings from the yellow foam. Paint one side of all the shapes with the orange fabric paint, ensuring you have a mirrored pair. Leave to dry.

TO MAKE THE WINGS

3 Using the score line on the template as a guide, very gently score a line on the inside of each wing at the base. This will allow you to bend the foam, creating two tabs with which to attach the wing to the cardigan.

Step 3

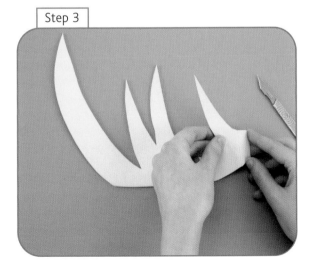

4 Lay two of the wings on the table yellow side up and paint a layer of fabric adhesive on both, avoiding the tab that will be used to attach the wings to the cardigan. Place one piece of red organza on top of each wing, pulling taut before pressing in place. Add a layer of orange organza, then the last piece of red. Allow the adhesive to seep through all three layers of fabric.

5 Brush a small amount of adhesive onto the second pair of wings and position on top of the first pair. Leave to dry. Trim the organza at the top of the wings.

6 Using a small pair of scissors cut away the two red layers of the organza at the bottom of the wings so that they are shorter than the orange layer—this will make the color look graded. Cut the edges of the orange layer in a gentle curve.

TO MAKE THE SPINE AND TAIL

7 Gently score a very shallow and straight line on the yellow side of the spine and tail piece as indicated on the template. Fold the spine shape in half leaving the tail part unfolded.

8 Mark a line on the cardigan all the way up the spine and along the center back of the hood to the peak.

9 Starting around 3 in. back from the front edge of the hood, begin basting one side of the spine in place along the stitch line marked on the template, also following the center back line marked on the cardigan. Use large hand stitches.

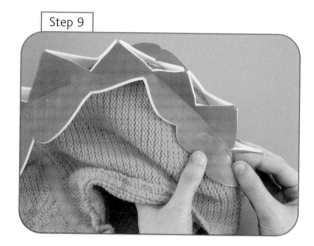

Step 9

10 Repeat for the other side, pushing the two edges up against one another causing the spinal ridges to stand up straight.

11 Try the cardigan on the child to find the best position for the wings. Mark with a pin, then remove the cardigan and sew the wings on in the same way as you attached the spine, stitching along the stitch lines marked on the template.

12 When everything is sewn in place, pipe a small amount of fabric adhesive in between the cardigan and the foam everywhere you have stitched. Leave to dry overnight.

Step 12

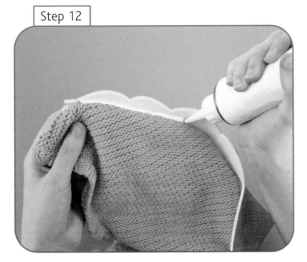

FROG

YOU WILL NEED

To fit a child of around 2 years

- Pair of white cotton leggings to fit child
- White cotton T-shirt to fit child
- Pair of white cotton socks to fit child
- Pair of white cotton socks to fit a six-year-old child
- 10 in. of 60-in.-wide white jersey
- Dylon machine dye in Lime
- 10 in. of 60-in.-wide mid-green fleece
- Scissors
- Fabric adhesive
- 2 styrofoam balls, approx. 3 in. in diameter
- White acrylic primer
- Dylon fabric paint in Fluorescent Orange
- Needle and green thread
- 12 orange pom-poms
- One 8 x 12-in. sheet of ¼-in. orange foam
- Dressmaker's pins
- Clothes peg
- Steam iron

Tip: *Glue the tongue off to one side of the jersey hairband so it does not obstruct the child's view.*

80

1 Dye the leggings, T-shirt, all the socks, and jersey fabric lime green according to the manufacturer's instructions. Leave to dry.

TO MAKE THE FROG'S BODY

2 Cut seven circles in assorted sizes from the fleece. Using fabric adhesive, stick firmly at random over the T-shirt, applying the adhesive right to the edge so that there are no loose edges.

TO MAKE THE FROG'S FEET

3 Take the pair of socks to fit a six-year-old and turn inside out. Mark three narrow "V" shapes at the toe end of each sock, to divide the ends into three pointy toes. Stitch along the lines then trim away excess fabric.

Step 3

4 Turn right side out and sew a pom-pom on each point. Make a small hole for the child's thumb in one side of the heel, and a horizontal slash where the ball of the foot would sit. These socks are worn on the child's hands.

5 Take the other pair of socks and sew three pom-poms onto the end of each sock. These are worn on the child's feet.

81

TO MAKE THE HAIRBAND

6 Measure the circumference of your child's head. Trim the strip of jersey so it is a little shorter than the head circumference.

7 Paint the styrofoam balls with white primer, leave to dry, then color them with orange fabric paint. Leave to dry.

8 Cut two small horizontal slits in the jersey strip centering them on the length about 7 in. apart and about halfway across the width. They should be just big enough to allow around one third of the styrofoam balls to go through.

9 Turn the jersey over and glue all around the edges of the slits to hold the balls in position. Leave to dry overnight.

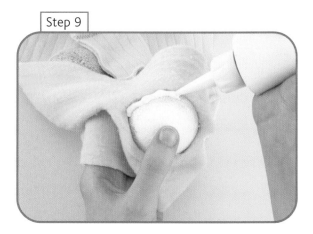

Step 9

10 With right sides together, stitch the two short ends of the headband together, then turn under along the long edges and hem together along the full length.

TO MAKE THE FROG'S TONGUE

11 Cut a narrow strip of foam sheet around 10 x ¼ in. Roll it up as tight as it will go and pin it in place. Hold the coiled foam with a peg. Take a hot steam iron, and direct steam toward the foam. This helps to curl the foam. Leave to cool.

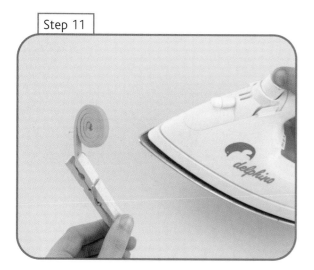

Step 11

12 Remove pins. Sew one end of the foam coil under the front edge of the hairband. Dab fabric adhesive on top of the stitching to reinforce it.

PEACOCK

YOU WILL NEED

To fit a child of around 11 months

- White cotton onesie with long sleeves, no legs, and no center front opening
- White cotton pull-on hat
- Dylon machine dye in Royal Blue
- Dressmaker's chalk
- 15-in. pieces of 54-in.-wide tulle in royal blue, turquoise, pale green, and pale blue
- Scissors
- Sheet of paper 10 x 40 in. (optional)
- Sewing machine
- 15-in. square piece of white silk habotai
- Dylon fabric paints in Turquoise, Royal Blue, Green, and Bronze
- Dylon Shade Creator
- Paintbrush
- Scrap of white fabric
- Iron
- Fabric adhesive
- 4 mini blue pom-poms

Tip: *It is much easier to cut tulle if you pair it with a piece of paper when cutting.*

1 Dye the onesie and hat blue according to the manufacturer's instructions. Leave to dry.

2 Mark a curved line with chalk on the seat of the onesie approx. one third of the way up from the crotch seam—this is where you will stitch the first row of tulle.

TO MAKE THE PEACOCK FEATHERS

3 Cut eight strips of tulle each 40 in. long, two from each color. Make the first strip 8 in. wide, then decrease the width of each strip by $3/4$ in. so the last is $2^3/4$ in. wide. Switch to a different color of tulle every time you decrease the width. It is easier to mark all the lines out on a piece of paper first, then lay the tulle over it and follow the lines when cutting.

4 Pair the strips together in descending size, the 8-in.-wide with the $7^1/4$-in.-wide and so on. Run a gathering stitch through both layers along one edge and gather to the length of the curved line on the onesie. When you have finished you should have four sets of gathered tulle.

5 Machine stitch the widest set of tulle along the curved line on the onesie with a $3/8$-in. seam, using a zigzag stitch. Position the set with the raw edges pointing toward the crotch, and with the wider tulle next to the onesie fabric.

Step 5

6 Repeat step 5 three more times, ending with the narrowest set of tulle. Remove the gathering threads after each strip has been applied.

7 Using the fabric paints, paint eight large and eight small egg-shaped outlines in green on the habotai.

8 Fill the outline with bronze, leaving an unpainted oval where the yolk would be on an egg. Fill this area with turquoise and royal blue, using the Shade Creator according to the manufacturer's instructions to create a shaded color. Leave to dry then iron the habotai under a scrap of fabric.

9 Cut out all the eggs and glue securely to the widest strip of the tulle fan, using liberal amounts of fabric adhesive.

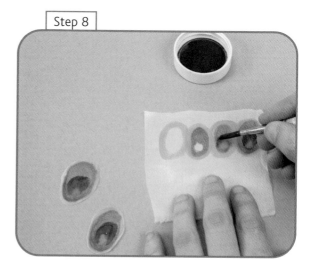

Step 8

TO MAKE THE HAT

10 Cut a piece of pale blue tulle 5½ x 2 in. and fold in half lengthwise. Stitch both short ends closed so that you have a long, narrow pocket.

11 Insert the small pom-poms into the pocket. Run a gathering stitch across the open side to close.

12 Pull the thread ends to gather the tulle into a semi-circle. Hand stitch the semi-circle to the top of the hat.

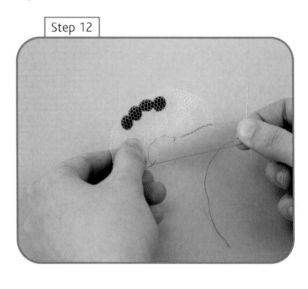

Step 12

FAIRY

YOU WILL NEED

To fit a child of around 2 years

- Dress of your choice to fit the child
- Two 24 x 24-in. sheets of ¼-in. blue foam
- Adhesive tape
- Tracing wheel
- Scalpel and cutting mat
- 1¼ yd. of 45-in.-wide sheer fabric printed with leaves or flowers
- Scissors
- PVA adhesive
- Paintbrush
- Hole punch
- Masking tape
- 2¼ yd. of ½-in.-wide purple ribbon

Tip: *If you cannot get a sheer fabric with a symmetrical design, you may have to cut the left and right sides of the fairy wings from the fabric in separate pieces to get the pattern symmetrical.*

1 Enlarge the template on page 140 so that it is 11½ in. across. Tape it down on a sheet of the foam, keeping it at one end so you can flip it over along the dotted line to make the second half of the wing. Using a tracing wheel, trace all the solid lines onto the foam. Do not trace along the dotted line.

2 Flip the template over along the dotted line to create the other half of the wing. Using a tracing wheel trace the solid lines. You now have a pair of wings. Cut round the outline then cut out the area unshaded on the template with the scalpel.

3 Now place your pair of wings directly onto your second sheet of foam and, using them as a template, copy the design, then cut out. You now have two pairs of wings.

4 Lay the sheer fabric on a table and move a pair of wings over to it to decide where the pattern of leaves or flowers looks best.

5 Paint the wrong side of one pair of wings sparingly with adhesive—just enough to make it tacky—excluding the area shaded dark gray on the template.

6 Pull the fabric taut and lay it on the wing, then leave the adhesive to dry. Mix one part adhesive with five parts water and paint the area of the fabric between the top and bottom sections of the wing. This will stiffen the fabric and prevent it from fraying. Cut around the design on the fabric to create an interesting edge to the wing.

Step 6

7 Trim away any excess fabric from the edge of the foam, using a scalpel. Glue the other pair of foam wings on top, but don't glue the area shaded dark gray on the template. Leave to dry.

8 There is now a section of wing that is still in two layers and is hanging free on both sides. Using the template as a guide, pull the right side of one layer back and match notches A to B. Glue in place and secure with a pin until dry. Repeat on the left side. This is now the back of the wing.

Step 8

9 The free section on the other layer will wrap round to lace up at the front. Using a hole punch, make six holes along the straight edge of this section on both sides. Then make two holes at center back at the top of the wings, where indicated on the template.

10 Wrap a small amount of masking tape around the ends of the ribbon to help push them through the holes. Starting at the back of the wings, push each end through one hole, so that ribbon is also providing shoulder support for the wings. Don't lace up until child is in costume.

Step 10

11 Paint over some of the design on a piece of spare fabric with the adhesive and water mix. When dry, cut out leaves or flowers and stitch or glue them to the wings and to the child's dress randomly. You can also stitch one to a hair clip.

12 To reinforce the waist section, you can cut another layer just of the dark gray shaded area of the template and glue that on top of the existing waist section.

ROBOT

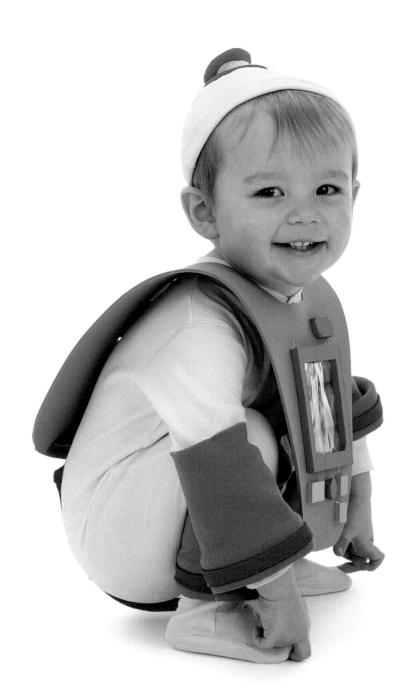

YOU WILL NEED

To fit a child of around 2 years

- White cotton onesie with long sleeves and legs, and center front opening
- White cotton pull-on hat
- Dylon machine dye in Sunflower
- One 12 x 17-in. sheet of ¼-in. blue foam
- Scalpel and cutting mat
- One 8 x 12-in. sheet of ¼-in. red foam
- One 8 x 12-in. sheet of ¼-in. green foam
- Fabric adhesive
- One 8 x 12-in. sheet of clear plastic (optional)
- One computer-printed picture (optional)
- Steam iron
- 10 in. of hook-and-loop tape
- 10 in. of 60-in.-wide red jersey
- 27 in. of 50-in.-wide blue felt
- One yellow pom-pom

Tip: *For the screen on the front of the tabard, you can either draw your own picture, or you can print one out from a computer.*

1 Dye the onesie and hat yellow according to the manufacturer's instructions. Leave to dry.

TO MAKE THE TABARD

2 Enlarge the tabard template on page 141 so that it is 22 in. at the longest point, and use to cut out the tabard from the blue foam sheet.

3 To make the computer screen, stick the computer-printed picture onto the front of the tabard. Cut a frame to fit it from the red foam. Cut a piece of the clear plastic to fit. Glue the frame onto the plastic. When dry, stick the frame, clear plastic side down, over the picture.

4 Cut some foam shapes to make buttons and toggles and glue them onto the tabard.

5 Holding the steam iron a safe distance away, direct a jet of steam at the shoulders of the tabard so it curves to fit over the shoulders. Hold the foam in this curved shape until it cools.

6 Cut a small square from both parts of the hook-and-loop tape. Cut a strip of red jersey about 2 x 8 in., making sure the stretch runs along the length. Stitch one square of hook-and-loop tape at one end and glue the matching square inside the front bottom of the tabard. Stitch the other end of the jersey strip inside the back bottom of the tabard to make a strip that goes between the child's legs to hold the tabard in place. Add a drop of fabric adhesive to secure the stitches.

TO MAKE THE CUFFS

7 Enlarge the templates on page 141 so that they are approx. 9½ in. at their longest point. Cut two wrist and two ankle cuffs from the blue felt.

8 Cut four strips of blue foam around 2 in. wide and to fit the circumference of each cuff. Stitch a strip on the bottom of each cuff on the inside. Leave 1 in. from each side seam free of foam so that you can sew up the seam. Sew cuffs shut. The foam will help kick the cuffs out into a circle.

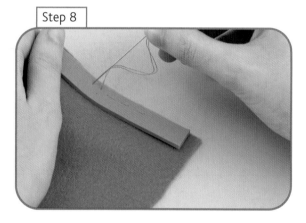

Step 8

9 Cut four strips of red jersey approx. 12 x 1 in. and glue one around the outside bottom of each cuff.

10 Handstitch the ankle cuffs onto the onesie, just below the knees, only catching the onesie at four points round each leg so it has room to stretch as the child moves. Repeat for the wrist cuffs, positioning them just below the elbow.

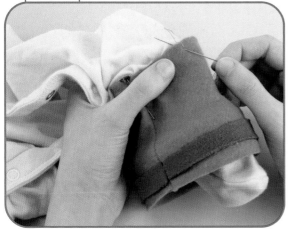

Step 10

TO MAKE THE HAT

11 Cut a spiral 3½ in. in diameter from the blue foam. Pull the spiral out and glue the pom-pom inside. Stitch the outer circle of the spiral to the top of the hat.

Step 11

PORCUPINE

YOU WILL NEED

To fit a child of around 11 months

- White cotton onesie with long sleeves and legs, and center front opening
- White cotton baseball hat with no markings on peak
- Dylon machine dye in Grey
- ¾ yd. of 62-in.-wide faux fur fabric
- Dressmaker's chalk
- Scissors
- Scalpel and cutting mat
- One 8 x 12-in. sheet of ¼-in. black foam
- Fabric adhesive
- Dressmaker's pins
- Masking tape
- Needle and brown thread
- Enough scraps of batting or fabric to fill the baseball hat
- One black pom-pom

Tip: *When you have finished making this costume, remember to check very carefully around the hems in the fur to make sure all the pins have been removed.*

1 Dye the onesie and hat gray according to the manufacturer's instructions. Leave to dry.

TO MAKE THE VEST

2 Enlarge the vest template on page 142 so that it is approx. 14½ in. along the straight edge. Place the template on the wrong side of the faux fur fabric, making sure the fur pile runs toward the base of the template. Draw around the outline with chalk and mark the quill holes as indicated by a "+" on the template. Flip the template over along the dotted line and draw the mirror image.

3 Cut out the vest. The best way to cut faux fur is from the back, using the tip of the scissors and making small snips to minimize damage to the fur. Alternatively, use a scalpel.

4 For the quills, cut 6-in.-long triangles, about ⅜ in. wide at the base, from the black foam.

5 Using the scalpel, cut a small slit ⅜ in. long at each quill hole marked on the back of the faux fur vest. Insert the pointed end of the quill and push through the fur until only ½ in. is left on the back.

6 Fold the square end of the quill over and glue to the back of the faux fur, holding it in place with a piece of masking tape until the adhesive dries. After removing the tape, reinforce with a couple of stitches.

Step 6

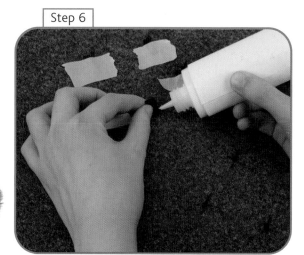

7 Turn under a hem of about ⅝ in. around the neck, fronts, and hem of the vest and either stick with fabric adhesive or hand stitch in place. If you use adhesive, hold the hem in place with pins until dry.

8 Turn under a hem of about ⅝ in. round the armholes and stitch in place.

TO MAKE THE HAT

9 Enlarge the hat template on page 142 so that it is approx. 11 in. across and cut the shape from the faux fur as advised in step 3. Using the ear template on page 136, cut four ear shapes from the faux fur. When you lay the templates out, make sure the pile of the fur runs toward the base of the templates.

10 Place two ear shapes right sides together and stitch all round the curved edge, then turn the ear right side out. Repeat for the other ear.

11 Fill the baseball cap with scraps of batting or fabric so it holds its shape while you work. Lay the fur shape over the cap so one of the seams is at center front and check the pile runs smoothly.

12 Mark on the cap where the side seams will fall. Remove the fur and stitch the ears onto the cap at either side where the seams are marked.

13 Lay the fur on the hat again and begin gluing down one section at a time. Pin in place until dry. It is best to do one section at a time, allowing it to dry thoroughly before starting the next section.

Step 13

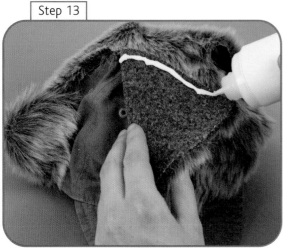

14 Bend the peak of the hat so that it ends in a point, then glue the black pom-pom onto the tip.

CABBAGE

YOU WILL NEED

To fit a child of around 3 months

- 40 in. of 45-in.-wide white brushed cotton
- Dylon machine dye in Lime and Deep Violet
- White cotton onesie with long sleeves, no legs, and no center front opening
- Approx. 4 safety pins
- Natural unbleached household string
- Bucket
- Dowel long enough to sit across bucket
- Rubber gloves
- Apron
- Newsprint
- Dylon hand dye in Deep Violet
- Glass measuring jug
- Stainless steel spoon
- Iron
- Rubber bands
- Scissors
- Needle and purple thread
- 1-lb. bag of polyester fiberfill stuffing

Tip: *Be careful not to splash the dye and don't use any plastic equipment with it as this will be permanently stained.*

1 Dye the cotton lime green and the onesie violet (with the machine dye) according to the manufacturer's instructions. Leave to dry.

2 Wet the cotton and wring slightly. Fold it in half lengthwise so raw edges meet. Fold in half again so folded edge meets raw edges. You now have four layers.

3 Lay the folded cotton on a table and make sure the fold and the raw edges line up. Now fold each end of the length of cotton to the middle and fold it in half. You will now have two folds on one side and one fold and two edges on the other.

4 Push a safety pin through the two folds catching all the layers. Repeat with another three safety pins, spacing them out along the fold line. Thread a piece of string through each safety pin and tie it to the dowel. Check that around half the fabric will hang in the bucket when the dowel is balanced across the top, then set the prepared fabric aside.

5 Wear rubber gloves and an apron and cover surfaces with newsprint. Mix the hand dye according to the manufacturer's instructions and add to the bucket.

6 Holding the ends of the dowel, gently lower the fabric into the dye bath until the dowel lies across the top of the bucket. About half the fabric should be submerged. Leave for an hour.

7 After one hour, put on the rubber gloves and apron again. Carefully remove the cotton from the dye and rinse in cold water until the water runs clear. Cover the ironing board with an old towel then quickly iron the damp fabric to get rid of creases, but not enough to dry it out.

8 To antique pleat the cotton you will need another person to help you. To protect the floor, put down newsprint, hold one long edge of the cotton taut between you, with the purple stripes perpendicular to the ground. Start pinching up ¼-in. pleats along the length of the cotton, keeping it taut at all times to ensure the pleats run along the full length.

9 When the cotton is all pleated, start to twist it while your helper twists in the opposite direction, so the cotton tightens and then curls into coils. Excess water will drip out as the fabric tightens. Fasten the coils with rubber bands and leave to dry overnight.

Step 9

TO MAKE THE CABBAGE BED

10 Uncoil the cotton and lay it flat. Enlarge the template on page 141 so that it is approx. 13½ in. across, then cut six large cabbage leaves, making sure one long edge is purple and the rest is green. Run a gathering stitch along the purple edge of each leaf and pull up to gather.

11 Measure from the neck to the crotch on the onesie. Cut two oval shapes from the purple part of the cotton this length and press flat.

12 Lay one oval on a table right side up and begin pinning the gathered edges of the cabbage leaves around the edge of the oval, all with right sides uppermost. Point the leaves toward the center of the oval—their edges should overlap each other.

13 Cut a slit 4 in. long in the center of the second oval, then lay it right side down on top of the first oval so the cabbage leaves are sandwiched between the two ovals. Stitch around the edge of the ovals, catching both ovals and all the leaves.

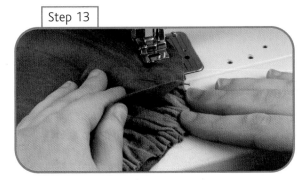

Step 13

14 Turn the cabbage bed right side out through the slit. Stuff the oval with fiberfill stuffing through the slit to make a cushion, then hand stitch the slit closed.

TO MAKE THE CABBAGE ROSETTE

15 Enlarge the template on page 141 again, this time to three different sizes: $4\frac{1}{2}$, 5, and $6\frac{1}{2}$ in. across. Cut a few leaves in each size, making sure that one curved edge is green and the rest is purple. Also cut a circle around 3 in. in diameter.

16 Run a gathering stitch around the purple edge of the leaves and pull up to gather. Start stitching the gathered edge of the small leaves to the circle, starting at the center with the smallest leaves.

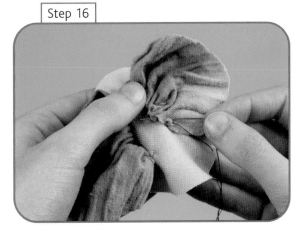

Step 16

17 Keep sewing leaves round the circle toward the edge, trying to put the largest and greenest on the outside. Leave the last $\frac{3}{8}$ in. of the circle free—sew through this edge to stitch the cabbage to the center front of the onesie.

TOADSTOOL

YOU WILL NEED

To fit a child of around 12 months

- White cotton onesie with long sleeves and legs, and center front opening
- Dylon machine dye in Sunflower
- 18-in. square of pale blue-gray felt
- Scissors
- Dylon fabric paint in Yellow
- 6-in. square scrap of plain cotton fabric
- Iron
- 1¾ yd. of 1¼-in.-wide yellow bias binding
- 60 in. of plastic boning strip
- Sewing machine
- Masking tape
- Needle and pale blue thread
- Pair of thick yellow panty hose

Tip: *Make your toadstool even brighter by using bright red felt and painting white circles onto it. Team the cap with a plain white onesie.*

1 Dye the onesie yellow according to the manufacturer's instructions. Leave to dry.

TO MAKE THE CAP

2 Cut a circle 16 in. in diameter from the blue-gray felt. Paint three large circles randomly on the felt with yellow fabric paint. Allow to dry then cover with the scrap of fabric and press with a hot iron to set, following the manufacturer's instructions.

3 Measure the circumference of the felt circle, then cut a length of bias binding the same length and a length of plastic boning strip around 6 in. shorter.

4 Stitch one edge of the bias binding along the edge of the felt circle. Stitch the other edge down, leaving the ends open so you can insert the plastic boning.

Step 4

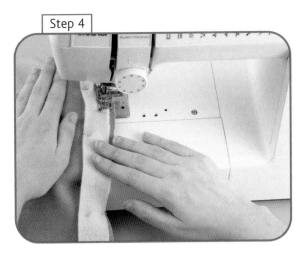

5 Cover the end of the plastic boning with masking tape so that you have a soft end to push through. Push the boning all the way round the brim of the cap.

6 When the boning has been pushed all the way round, overlap the two ends by approx. 4 in. and either sew or tape together. Push back in and distribute the gathers evenly. Trim excess cap fabric.

Step 6

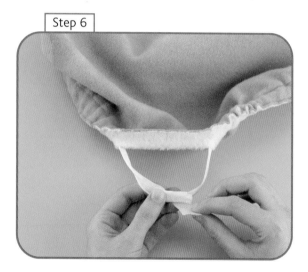

7 Cut off the legs of the panty hose in a straight line. Hand stitch the trimmed edge of the rest of the panty hose onto the underside of the toadstool cap. Position it to one side so that when the toadstool cap is worn, the bulk of it will fall behind the child's head.

Step 7

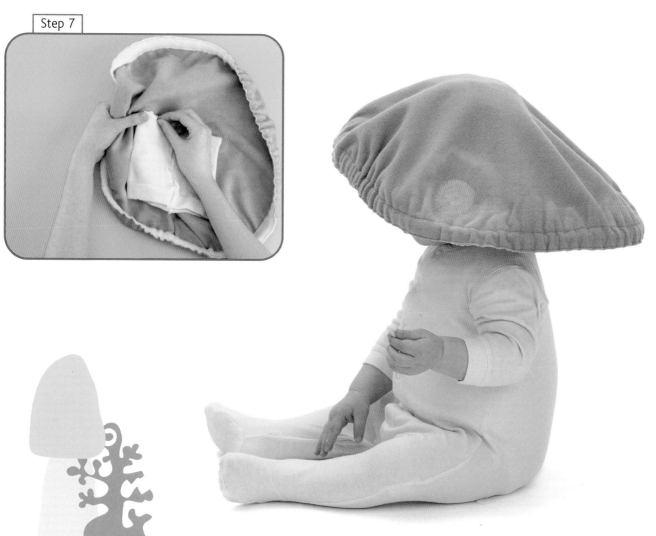

FLOWERBUD

YOU WILL NEED

To fit a child of around 10 months

- White cotton onesie with no sleeves or legs, and no center front opening
- 1¼ yd. of 72-in.-wide white felt, cut into three equal pieces along the width
- Dylon hand dye in Baby Pink, Deep Pink, Green, and Dark Green
- Scissors
- Fabric adhesive
- Sewing machine
- Dressmaker's pins
- 20 in. of ¼-in.-wide elastic
- 8 in. of green hook-and-loop tape

Tip: *You can arrange the flower petals any way you like by gluing some of them to the onesie at the tip, or letting them fall naturally.*

1 Dye the onesie and one piece of the felt pale pink according to manufacturer's instructions. Leave to dry.

2 Dye one piece of the felt deep pink according to the manufacturer's instructions. Leave to dry.

3 Divide the remaining piece of felt in half and dye one half green and the other dark green according to the manufacturer's instructions. Leave to dry.

4 Enlarge the petals template on page 142 so that the length is approx. 19 in. and cut two rows of petals from the deep pink felt and two rows from the pale pink felt.

5 Enlarge the template on page 143 so that it is approx. 22 in. at the longest point. Cut along the outside line on the template to make a diaper-shaped bud from green felt. Cut along the inside line on the template to make a second bud in dark green. Glue the two layers together, leave to dry, then top stitch approx. ¾ in. from the edges.

6 Pleat each row of pink petals along the straight edge and pin to hold. Ensure the length of the pleated edge is slightly larger than the width of the onesie.

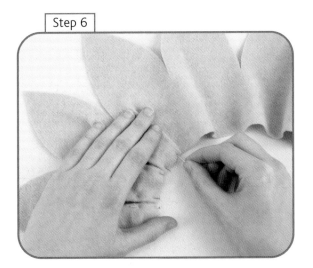

Step 6

7 Lay one row of dark pink petals on the onesie from side seam to side seam in a straight line, around ½ in. above the leg hole. Machine stitch in place using a zigzag stitch, slightly stretching the onesie as you work to match the length of the petal row.

8 Repeat with the other row of dark pink petals on the back of the onesie. The onesie should still stretch enough to fit over your child's head and shoulders.

9 Repeat steps 7 and 8 with the rows of pale pink petals, positioning them around ⅜ in. below the large row.

10 If the petals flop when you hold the onesie up by the shoulders then fix some of the petals onto the onesie with a small drop of fabric adhesive. Bend the petals a small amount to stop the onesie from straining when the child is moving around in the costume.

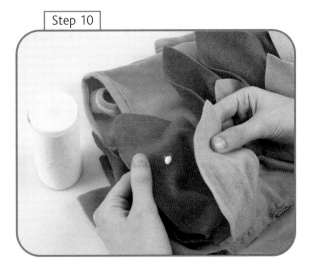

Step 10

11 Cut two lengths of elastic around 1½ in. shorter than the leg hole of the green felt diaper. Stitch a length of elastic around each leg hole, as marked on the template, using a wide zigzag stitch and stretching the elastic as you work.

12 Using the template as a guide, sew hook-and-loop tabs on the inside of the diaper. Make sure the softer side of the hook-and-loop is attached to the back so there is no chance of the child being scratched.

Step 12

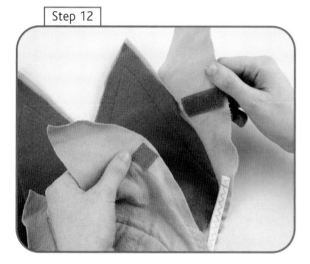

DRAGONFLY

YOU WILL NEED

To fit a child of around 3 years

- White cotton onesie with long sleeves and legs, and center front opening
- ¾ yd. of 60-in.-wide white jersey, with one 2 x 35-in. strip cut off
- Dylon machine dye in Yellow
- Dylon fabric dye in Vivid Turquoise
- ¾ yd. of 60-in.-wide metallic pale green fabric
- ½ yd. of 60-in.-wide metallic dark blue fabric
- ½ yd. of 60-in.-wide metallic blue fabric
- Scissors
- Sewing machine
- Iron
- ½ yd. of lightweight batting
- Needle and blue and black thread
- Dressmaker's pins
- Small piece of hook-and-loop tape
- Adult-sized turquoise fishnet panty hose
- 1-lb. bag of polyester fiberfill stuffing
- Two 8 x 12-in. sheets of ¼-in. blue foam
- Two 8 x 12-in. sheets of ¼-in. green foam
- Scalpel and cutting mat
- Paintbrush
- Fabric adhesive
- ½ yd. of 45-in.-wide green organza
- ½ yd. of 45-in.-wide blue organza

1 Dye the onesie and jersey strip yellow according to the manufacturer's instructions. Leave to dry.

2 Dye the remaining jersey turquoise according to the manufacturer's instructions. Leave to dry.

TO MAKE THE TABARD

3 Cut a strip 5 in. wide across the full width of the pale green metallic fabric.

4 With right sides together, machine stitch the width of dark blue metallic fabric on one side of the pale green and the light blue on the other. Press the seams open on the reverse. You now have a large piece of fabric with three stripes. Reserve the rest of the pale green fabric for the tail.

5 Enlarge the tabard template on page 143 so that it is 15½ in. at the longest point. Cut two tabard shapes from the jersey, the batting, and the striped fabric. When placing the template on the striped fabric, make sure you get the stripes in the same position each time.

6 Lay a piece of batting on the back of one of the striped pieces, matching the edges. Baste together round all the edges. Repeat for the other piece of batting and striped fabric.

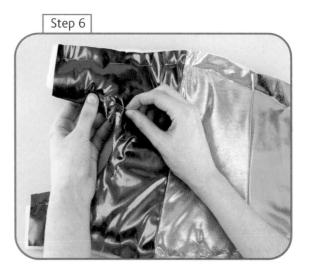

Step 6

7 With striped sides together, stitch the shoulder seams through the striped fabric and batting. Trim excess batting from the seams and press them open.

8 Stitch the shoulder seams on the pieces of jersey and press them open. Lay the jersey tabard on top of the striped one, with right sides together and matching the edges.

9 Sew around the edges of the tabard, but leave the neck open. Turn the tabard right side out through the neck opening.

10 Trim the batting back by ¹/₂ in. from the edge of the neck. Turn the edge of the striped fabric over the edge of the batting and pin in place from the outside.

11 Turn the neck edge of the jersey in by ¹/₄ in. and pin in place from the outside. Slip stitch around the neck hole to hold the jersey and striped fabric together. Remove all the pins.

Step 11

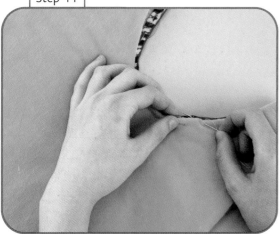

12 Measure the distance between the front and the back of the tabard between the child's legs. Add 3 in. to the measurement then cut a strip of jersey to this length, and 2 in. wide.

13 Stitch one piece of hook-and-loop tape to the end of the jersey strip and the matching half inside the front of the tabard, near the bottom. Stitch the other end of the jersey strip to the back of the tabard, around 1 in. from the bottom.

TO MAKE THE TAIL

14 Cut a strip of green metallic fabric 12 x 48 in. and fold in half lengthwise with right sides together. Stitch across one short end and down the long edge.

15 Turn the tube of metallic fabric right side out. Push your hand inside the tube, and grasping the end, slide the tube into one leg of the panty hose, right to the toe.

16 Slide your hand out again, leaving the fabric tube inside the panty hose. Fill the fabric tube with fiberfill stuffing, then trim the leg of the panty hose back to the top of the tube.

17 Wrap lengths of black thread round the tube at around 8-in. intervals, and tie off neatly. Stitch the top of the tube inside the back of the tabard.

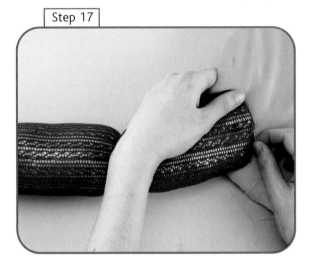
Step 17

TO MAKE THE WINGS

18 Enlarge the wing template on page 143 so that it is approx. 12 in. long. Cut two from the blue foam and two from the green, using a scalpel. You are making a left-hand pair of wings and a right-hand pair: each pair has blue foam at the front and green foam at the back.

19 Cut two pieces of blue organza and two pieces of green, each 8 x 12 in.

20 Lay the blue foam wing shapes down side by side in a mirror image and brush lightly with adhesive so the surface is just tacky.

21 Place a layer of blue organza onto the top two wing pieces, laying the bottom raw edge of the fabric along the top edge of the wing.

22 Place a layer of green organza onto the bottom two wing pieces, laying the bottom raw edge of the fabric along the top edge of the wing.

23 Brush a small amount of adhesive onto the green foam wing shapes and place on top of the blue wing pieces, matching all edges. Leave to dry, then trim the excess off the edges and cut the bottom edges of organza in a straight line.

24 Lay the wings on the back of the onesie approx. 6 in. apart and sew in place using a big basting stitch. Pipe adhesive underneath, between the layers, for extra reinforcement. The wings should be flat to the body so that the tabard can lie flat over the top.

CORNCOB

YOU WILL NEED

To fit a child of around 5 months

- White cotton onesie with long sleeves, no legs, and no center front opening
- 10 x 10-in. piece of white jersey, stretchy in both directions
- Dylon machine dye in Sunflower
- 2¼ yd. of 45-in.-wide white cotton fabric
- Dylon machine dye in Green
- Sewing machine
- Scissors
- 1-lb. bag of polyester fiberfill stuffing
- Needle and yellow thread
- Dylon fabric paints in Yellow, Gold, and Bronze
- Paintbrush
- 2¼ yd. of 50-in.-wide lightweight batting
- 6-oz. bag of yellow raffia
- Fabric adhesive

Tip: *When you sew the jersey onto the front of the onesie, be careful you don't catch the back layer of the onesie too.*

1 Dye the onesie and jersey yellow according to the manufacturer's instructions. Leave to dry.

2 Dye the cotton fabric green according to the manufacturer's instructions. Leave to dry.

TO MAKE THE CORN

3 Stitch the piece of jersey to the front layer of the onesie only, using fine zigzag stitch so the onesie will still stretch. Trim away the excess jersey along the stitching.

4 Still working only through the front layer of the onesie, stitch approx. four vertical lines evenly spaced down the piece of jersey and approx. four horizontal lines evenly spaced across it. Use a fine zigzag stitch so the onesie will still be stretchy.

Step 4

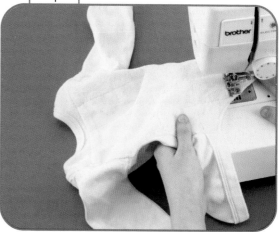

5 Turn the onesie inside out and make a small slit through the center of each stitched rectangle. Be careful to cut only the onesie fabric. Stuff each kernel generously through the slit, then hand stitch closed.

6 Turn the onesie right side out. Using the fabric paints, color the kernels in yellow, bronze, and gold. Color them randomly, leaving some unpainted. Leave to dry.

Step 5

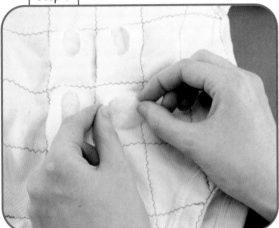

Step 6

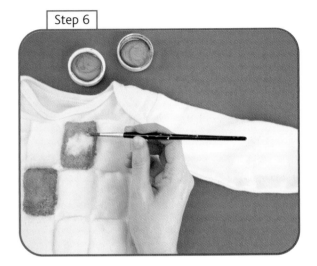

TO MAKE THE HUSK

7 Cut a circle with a 12-in. diameter from a corner of the batting. Enlarge the template on page 142 to 33$\frac{1}{2}$ in. long and 9$\frac{1}{2}$ in. wide at the base. Use it to cut three large husk shapes from the batting. Enlarge the same template to 23$\frac{1}{2}$ in. long and 9$\frac{1}{2}$ in. wide at the base and use it to cut two small husks.

8 Using the same templates, cut six large husk shapes and four small ones from the green fabric. Also cut two circles with a 13-in. diameter.

9 Pair up matching pieces of husk fabric and place each pair right sides together, with a matching piece of batting on top. Machine stitch round the edge of each set, pivoting the needle at the tip of the husk and leaving the base open.

10 Trim excess batting from the seam allowance. Turn the husk right side out through the opening at the base. Baste across the base line through the fabric and batting, about 1 in. from the raw edge.

11 Trim the batting back inside the seam allowance at the base. Top stitch lines along the husk from the basting line at the base to the tip, spacing them 1$\frac{1}{2}$ in. apart at the base and converging at the tip.

12 Lay the circles of fabric on top of one another, wrong sides together, and sandwich the circle of batting between them. Baste around the edge.

13 Overlap the large husk shapes along one edge of the circle, with right sides together. Machine stitch in place through all layers then flip the husks over to the other side so all the seam allowances are inside where the child will sit.

14 Attach small husks in the same way, but hand stitch them to the base along the opposite side.

15 Shape the husks to form a cradle then stitch them together by hand to hold them in place. Stitch at least two of the large husks right up to the tip.

16 Make a tuft of raffia and stitch to the tip of the pair of large husks. Pipe some fabric adhesive generously round the base of the raffia to make sure no strands will come out. Leave to dry.

LION

YOU WILL NEED

To fit a child of around 2 years

- White cotton onesie with long sleeves, no legs, and no center front opening
- Dylon machine dye in Burnt Orange
- Scissors
- ¼ yd. of 60-in.-wide yellow fleece
- ¼ yd. of 60-in.-wide yellow jersey
- ¼ yd. of 60-in.-wide tan faux suede
- 1-lb. bag of polyester fiberfill stuffing
- ¾ yd. of ½-in.-wide elastic
- Needle and yellow thread
- 1¼ yd. of brown marabou trim
- 12 in. of thin cord

Tip: *It is important to give the marabou trim enough slack when stitching it on, so it doesn't snap when the child moves around.*

1 Dye the onesie orange according to the manufacturer's instructions. Leave to dry.

TO MAKE THE HAIRBAND

2 Cut strips from the fleece, jersey, and faux suede, each 9 in. long and with varying widths from 3 to 5 in. Do not use all the jersey as you will need some for the ears and tail.

3 Lay three colored strips one on top of another so that the widest is at the bottom and narrowest is at the top, matching center lines. Make enough for the hairband only at this stage.

4 Measure the circumference of your child's head. Cut a length of elastic to the same measurement.

5 Lay the elastic on top of the layered strips of fabric. Machine stitch, using a zigzag stitch, down the entire length, stretching the elastic as you work.

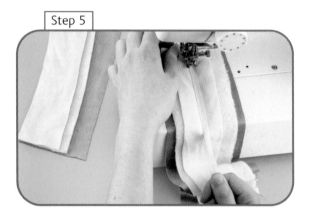

Step 5

6 When you have stitched the full length of the elastic, cut off any remaining fabric.

7 Using the template on page 136, cut four ears from the yellow jersey.

8 With right sides together, pair the ears up and stitch round the curved edge of each. Fill sparingly with stuffing.

9 Pinch the center of the raw edge together and stitch to hold in place then hand stitch the ears onto the elastic on each side of the hairband—the elastic should still be on top of the fabric strips.

10 Hand stitch a strip of marabou on top of the elastic to hide it—use loose stitches and allow a little slack in the marabou so it doesn't snap when the elastic is stretched.

11 Fray each layer of fabric with scissors by cutting into the jersey on both sides of the elastic and pulling on the jersey frays to create curls. Overlap ends of the elastic by approx. 1 in. and stitch together.

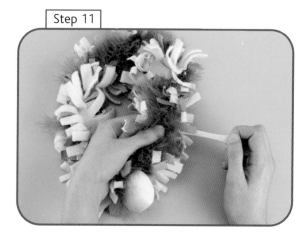

Step 11

TO MAKE THE CUFFS

12 Lay three more colored strips on top of one another so that they all meet up along one edge. Repeat with the remaining strips.

13 Place the strips with the widest on top. Place the remaining elastic along the top edge of the fabric and machine stitch in place with a zigzag stitch, stretching the elastic as you work.

14 Measure the circumference of your child's leg just below the knee. Cut two cuffs from the elastic-fabric lengths you have just made, the same length as this measurement.

15 Overlap the ends of the elastic and stitch together. The cuff will now be slightly too small so it will grip the leg and not fall down.

16 Attach the marabou trim as you did for the hairband in step 10 and fray the fabric strips as you did in step 11.

TO MAKE THE RUFF

17 The remaining fabric-elastic length is for the ruff. Pin elastic round the neck of the onesie, then stitch in place. Maintain the stretch in the onesie by using loose stitches and only catching it every so often.

Step 17

18 Sew marabou trim on top of stitch line. Allow enough marabou trim so that when the neckline is stretched the marabou trim doesn't snap.

19 Fray the edges of the fabric strips as you did in step 11.

TO MAKE THE TAIL

20 Cut a strip of yellow jersey approx. 10 x 3 in. Fold in half lengthwise, right sides together.

21 Place the length of cord between the two layers, pushing it right to the fold. Stitch over one short end to keep it in place, then stitch down the long edge, making sure not to catch the cord.

22 Pull on the cord, gently coaxing the tube to turn right side out. Remove the cord and stuff the tail with fiberfill stuffing so it is full but not stiff. Stitch some odd bits of frayed fabric onto the closed end and stitch the open end to the seat of the onesie.

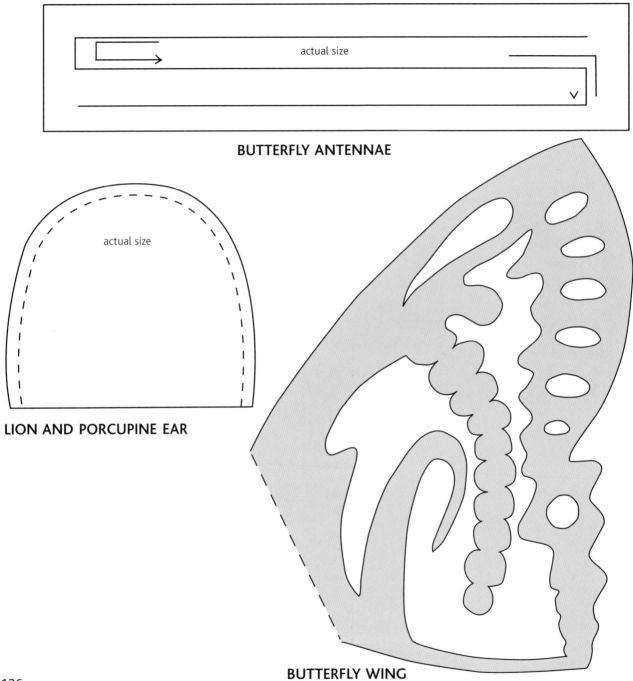

actual size

BUTTERFLY ANTENNAE

actual size

LION AND PORCUPINE EAR

BUTTERFLY WING

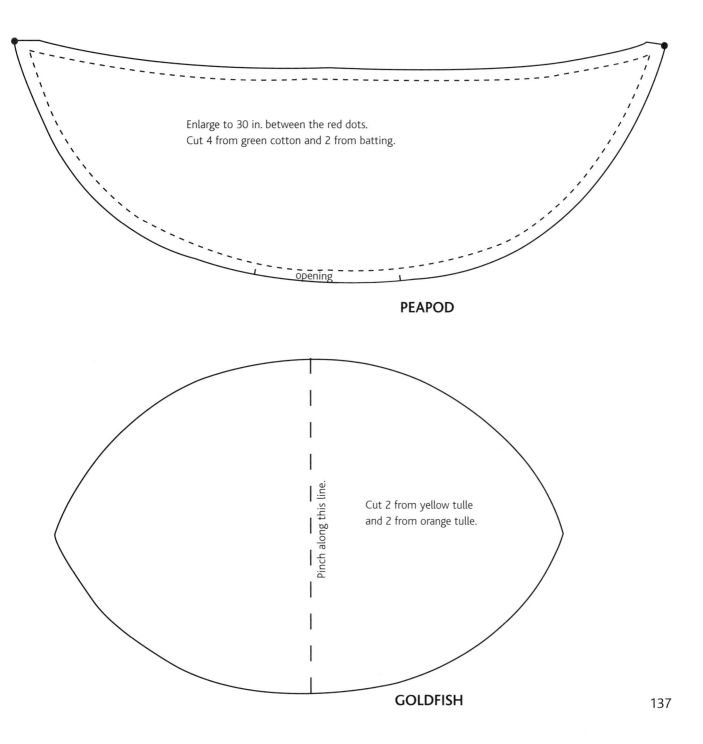

Enlarge to 30 in. between the red dots.
Cut 4 from green cotton and 2 from batting.

opening

PEAPOD

Pinch along this line.

Cut 2 from yellow tulle
and 2 from orange tulle.

GOLDFISH

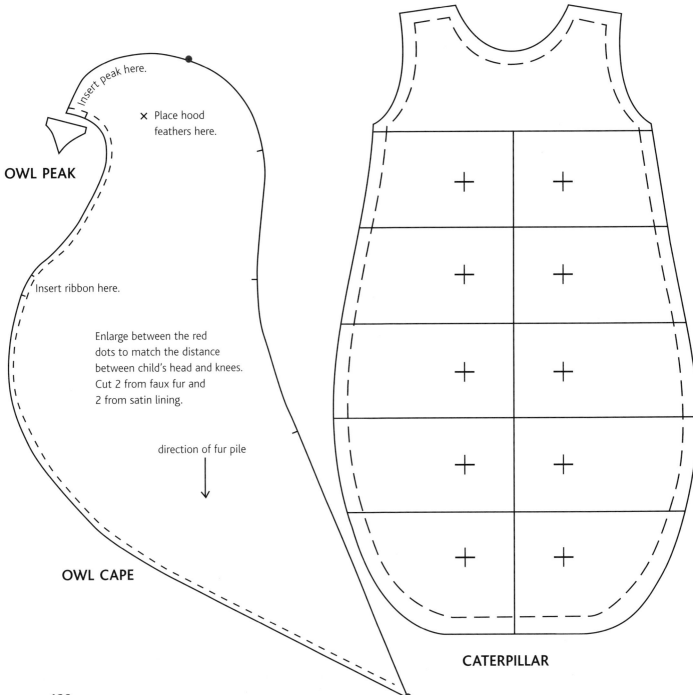

OWL PEAK

Insert peak here.

✕ Place hood feathers here.

Insert ribbon here.

Enlarge between the red dots to match the distance between child's head and knees. Cut 2 from faux fur and 2 from satin lining.

direction of fur pile

OWL CAPE

CATERPILLAR

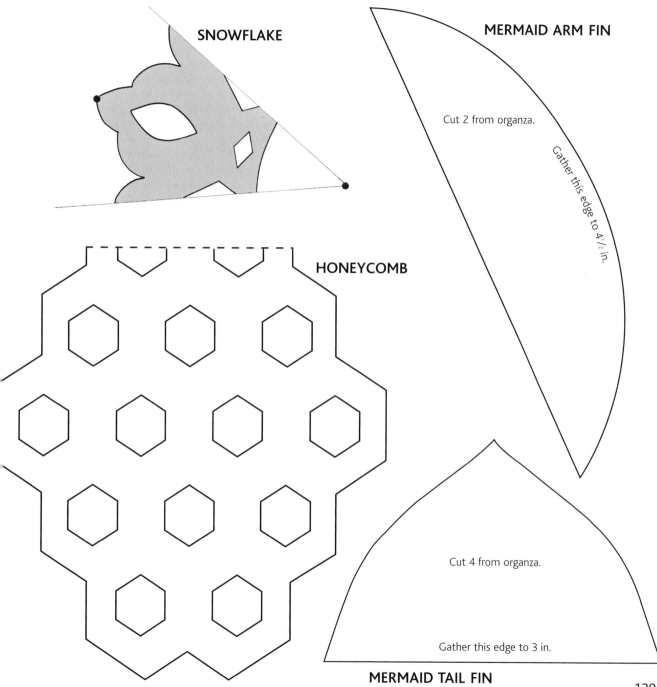

SNOWFLAKE

MERMAID ARM FIN

Cut 2 from organza.

Gather this edge to 4½ in.

HONEYCOMB

Cut 4 from organza.

Gather this edge to 3 in.

MERMAID TAIL FIN

139

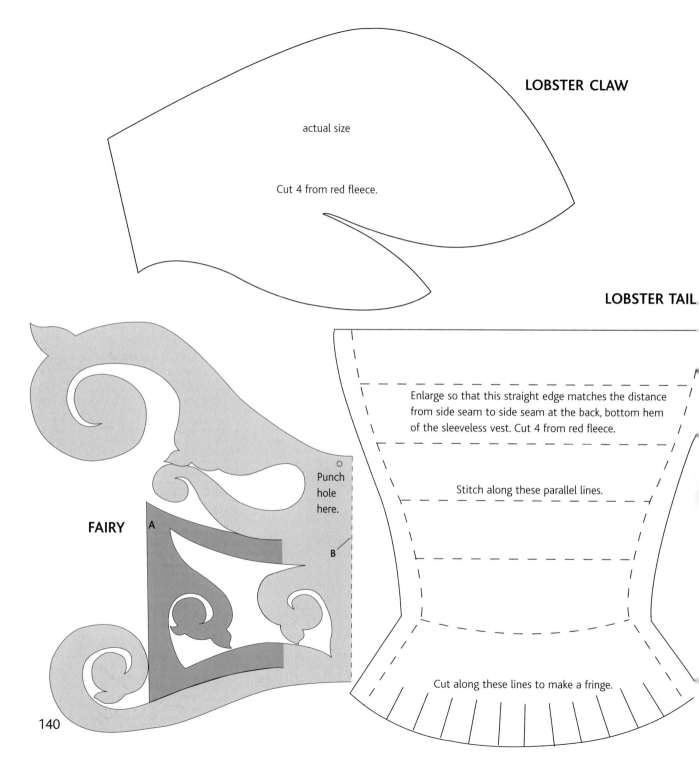

LOBSTER CLAW

actual size

Cut 4 from red fleece.

LOBSTER TAIL

Enlarge so that this straight edge matches the distance from side seam to side seam at the back, bottom hem of the sleeveless vest. Cut 4 from red fleece.

Stitch along these parallel lines.

Cut along these lines to make a fringe.

Punch hole here.

FAIRY

A

B

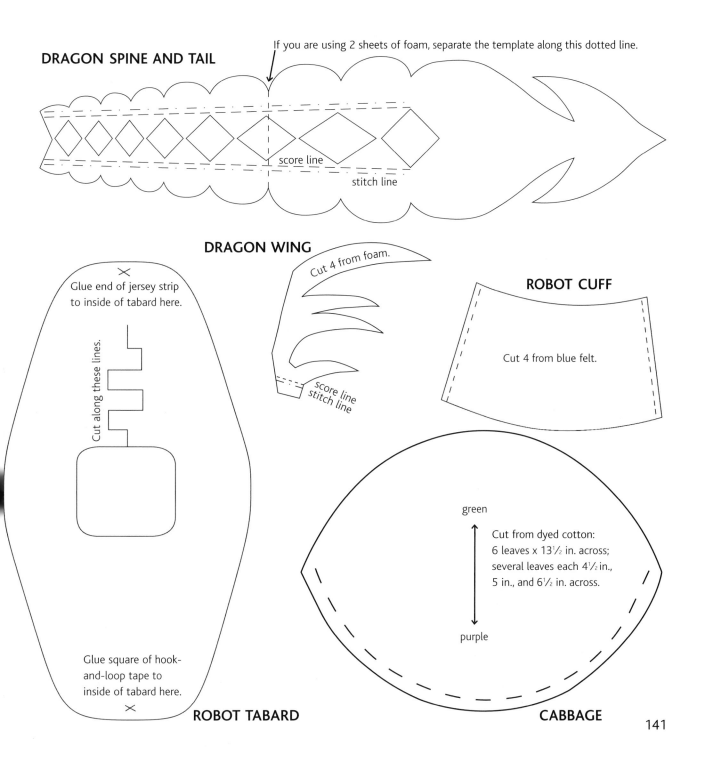

DRAGON SPINE AND TAIL

If you are using 2 sheets of foam, separate the template along this dotted line.

score line

stitch line

DRAGON WING

Cut 4 from foam.

score line
stitch line

Glue end of jersey strip to inside of tabard here.

Cut along these lines.

Glue square of hook-and-loop tape to inside of tabard here.

ROBOT TABARD

ROBOT CUFF

Cut 4 from blue felt.

green

Cut from dyed cotton: 6 leaves x 13½ in. across; several leaves each 4½ in., 5 in., and 6½ in. across.

purple

CABBAGE

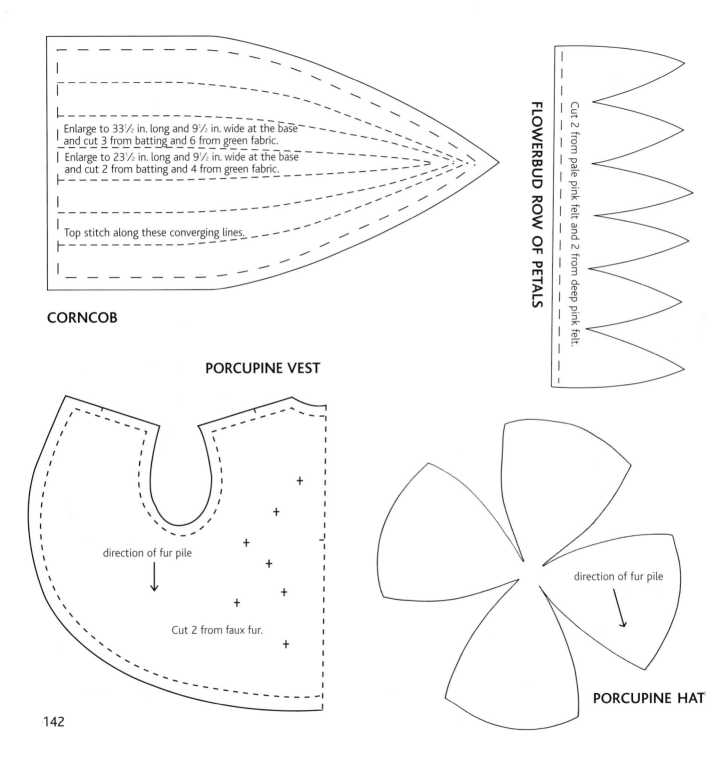

CORNCOB

Enlarge to 33½ in. long and 9½ in. wide at the base and cut 3 from batting and 6 from green fabric.

Enlarge to 23½ in. long and 9½ in. wide at the base and cut 2 from batting and 4 from green fabric.

Top stitch along these converging lines.

FLOWERBUD ROW OF PETALS

Cut 2 from pale pink felt and 2 from deep pink felt.

PORCUPINE VEST

direction of fur pile

Cut 2 from faux fur.

PORCUPINE HAT

direction of fur pile

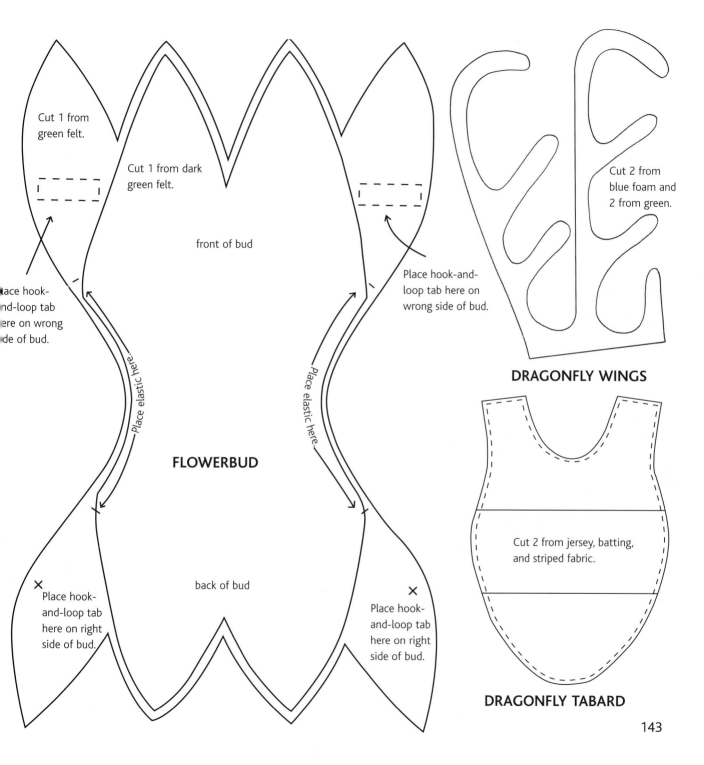

Cut 1 from green felt.

Cut 1 from dark green felt.

front of bud

Place hook-and-loop tab here on wrong side of bud.

Place hook-and-loop tab here on wrong side of bud.

Place elastic here.

Place elastic here.

FLOWERBUD

back of bud

× Place hook-and-loop tab here on right side of bud.

× Place hook-and-loop tab here on right side of bud.

DRAGONFLY WINGS

Cut 2 from blue foam and 2 from green.

DRAGONFLY TABARD

Cut 2 from jersey, batting, and striped fabric.

ACKnowledgments

MQ Publications would like to thank all the little stars who modeled costumes and made this book so lovely.

Jada Adeyemi-Jones
25 months
fairy, lion, snowflake

Fiona Madeleine Bell
11 weeks
peapod, cabbage

Jada-li Bowerman
24 months
flamingo, frog

Jack Goose
23 months
owl, robot, lobster

Mia Hart
10 months
mermaid, butterfly, flowerbud

Kike Lewis
5 months
caterpillar, corncob

Dylan Rook
3 years
solar system,
dragonfly

Charlie Smith
12 months
turtle, toadstool

Kamran Soneji
11 months
peacock, goldfish

Constance Thoms
11 months
honeycomb,
porcupine

Joseph Pablo Weil
15½ months
dragon